PRAISE FOR *STOP BREATHE BELIEVE*

"Dianne Morris Jones has written a compassionate and insightful guide-book for anyone who's struggled with times of stress, self-doubt, conflict, or grief—in other words, all of us. *Stop Breathe Believe* teaches a simple yet powerful mindfulness based practice that transforms our unhealthy thinking into healthy thinking, one thought at a time. Appropriate for all ages and applicable to any type of struggle, *Stop Breathe Believe* promotes healing of the mind, body, and spirit."

—Richard L. Deming, MD, Medical Director, Mercy Cancer Center; Founder and Chairman, Above + Beyond Cancer

"If you are in the overwhelming place and wondering, 'How will I ever move from this dark place to one of peace and empowerment?', then you have just found the right road map in *Stop Breathe Believe*. Dianne has provided us with the practical step by step guide to mindful living in a clear, personal, and touching way. This is the book for your journey to change!"

—Terry Hargrave, Ph.D., Professor of Marriage and Family Therapy, Fuller Theological Seminary and co-author of *Restoration Therapy: Guiding Understanding and Healing in Marriage and Family Therapy*

"To hold *Stop Breathe Believe* in your hands is like having a personal GPS tracker programmed to help you locate what is truly good and decent in life: the ground of being, a profound sense of peace, and hope in this moment. What appears to be a simple technique is actually a powerful means of recognizing negativity, cleansing it from the mind and body, and getting unstuck as you open to the realms of clarity, healing, wholeness, and possibility that are your human birthright. Unwrap this book as you would a gift—for Dianne has filled each page with inspiring stories and practical tools that will warm your heart, and align you with your purpose and your place on this planet. Highly recommended."

—Donald Altman, author of *One-Minute Mindfulness, The Mindfulness Toolbox, The Mindfulness Code,* and *Living Kindness*

"*Stop Breathe Believe* offers a straightforward, easy-to-understand and insightful method of facing hardship, tragedy, and tension. Dianne advocates stopping to regroup, relying on some means of steady support, and eventually, believing in life again. The latter is the thrust of the book. If you find yourself questioning your value, purpose, and abilities, *Stop Breathe Believe* will likely fill you with new energy and direction."

—Robyn Brammer, Ph.D., Assoc. Dean of Grad School, Central Washington University, author of *Diversity in Counseling*

"Engaging and useful. Grounded in solid cognitive behavioral principles that are demonstrated using meaningful, real-world examples. Jones offers practical tips and suggestions that are easy to remember and implement. It will make you see traffic signals in a whole new way. Stop...and be fully alive!"

—Ronda L. Dearing, Ph.D., Senior Research Scientist, University at Buffalo and co-editor of *Shame in the Therapy Hour*

STOP
BREATHE
BELIEVE

STOP
breathe
BELIEVE

Mindful Living One Thought at a Time

DIANNE MORRIS JONES, LMHC, CDWF-C
with Catherine Knepper

Illustrations by Monica N. Ghali

Cover artwork by Robert Spellman
Cover design, interior design, and typesetting by Monica N. Ghali
Back cover photo by Justin Salem Meyer

Author's Note

This publication is not intended as a substitute for the advice of health-care professionals.

Except in the case of my immediate family members and my friends Helen, Nancy, and Nawal, all names and identifying details have been changed in order to preserve client confidentiality. Dialogue is not a verbatim reproduction of what occurred in the counseling room, but written to the best of my recollection and to express the principles of Stop Breathe Believe®.

To Roger, Justin, Jill & Brent—

May you invite
each day,
each hour,
each moment
as a gift to live fully alive—

I love you!

TABLE *of* CONTENTS

INTRODUCTION
Almost a Miracle

Marla came to see me at the lowest point of her life. In the midst of a contentious divorce, she was behind on her bills and sleeping only a few hours a night. Her two teenage sons were starting to get in trouble at school, and she didn't have the emotional resources to be the mother she wanted to be. She was at her wits' end when she sat down in my office.

"I'm in a constant state of fear," she said. "I stay up all night worrying about everything that's going wrong and everything that *could* go wrong. I've got one worst-case scenario after another marching through my head, and I'm exhausted. I can't focus at work because my mind is constantly elsewhere…my boss has already called me in to discuss some stupid mistakes I made. And I absolutely cannot lose this job. But I can't be productive with my mind in such a fog, and I can't take time out for myself with so much pressure at work—I'm stuck."

Now let's take a glimpse ahead to several weeks later. Marla was still in the midst of a painful divorce and her youngest son was still failing geometry. But she'd paid the bills she could and started payment plans for the others, she was sleeping six to seven hours a night, and said she felt much calmer at work.

Now skip ahead to four *years* later, as Marla and I were ending our time together. The ugly divorce was behind her, her sons were both in college, and she was in a new and healthy relationship. We spent our last session reviewing and celebrating the progress she'd made. "Stop Breathe Believe was the key," she said. "I did a lot of hard work, but Stop Breathe Believe was the start of the positive change, and it's been the sustaining factor behind it too—and in the boys' lives! They're using Stop Breathe Believe at school, for everything from test anxiety to pre-game jitters. Daniel uses it like I do, as a way to start every day on the right foot. He says it's his own personal vaccine against negativity."

In the six years I've been teaching Stop Breathe Believe® in my private practice and in workshops, I've heard countless stories like Marla's. Not every story is as dramatic as hers, but I have yet to encounter someone who hasn't benefited from the regular practice of Stop Breathe Believe. The stories of how people have used Stop Breathe Believe to navigate and overcome some of life's most difficult challenges have convinced me that the practice is universally applicable and, if regularly used, can improve the lives of anyone who uses it.

So, what is it? Stop Breathe Believe is a tool anyone can learn to *stop* the self-defeating thoughts that prevent us from living authentically, *breathe* our way to a calmer and more grounded state of being, and *believe* in a compassionate self-talk statement that addresses our unique situation. At its simplest level, Stop Breathe Believe helps us stop unhealthy thinking in its tracks, slow down enough to breathe deeply and see the truth of a situation, and replace the thoughts that derail us with healthy thinking that directly improves our lives.

A staggering number of thoughts enter our minds on a daily basis, and every one of them exerts an effect on us. Whether you're worrying about your bank balance, or your kindergartener's first day of school, or your career advancement, or your teen's driving or choice of friends, or your frustration with what you eat, or your lack of discipline in getting to the gym, or giving an effective presentation at the board meeting, or problems communicating with your partner, or your failed relationship, or your future, or your past—we *all* struggle with our thoughts from time to time. And if our thoughts run amok, as Marla's were, we can find ourselves living at the mercy of them.

But the amazing truth is that we have the ability to *choose* which thoughts we allow in. It takes practice, but you can learn to say yes to constructive, healthy thoughts, and no to destructive, self-defeating thoughts.

The original idea for Stop Breathe Believe came to me during a time when I was really struggling. I was at a complicated point in my career in which I felt like I couldn't use my voice in a way that was true to my values and my faith and my deepest sense of my soul. My stomach ached, I cried, and intuitively I just felt out of alignment. I knew for my physical, mental and spiritual health that I needed to move on. The struggle was difficult because I loved my work and the people I worked with, and the prospect of leaving, necessary as it was, was heart wrenching. Then, at a conference, a speaker touched the core of my hurt when she spoke on the need to be true to the deep parts of your soul, and not to hide or be silent during conflict. It was a holy moment for me. I recall feeling the ache in my stomach lift as my mind and body agreed with the truth of her words. Right there, I made a resolution to be more honest with my voice, especially regarding the difficult issues.

To help sort through my thoughts and motivations and become more intentional with my thinking, I bought an inexpensive watch that I set to go off every hour on the hour. When the alarm went off, I would "catch" my thought. What was I thinking at that moment? Was I ruminating on a source of stress or worrying about things beyond my control? Was I experiencing a moment of gratitude, or was I focusing on a good intention? My goal was simply to become aware of my thought as the alarm went off, regarding it *without judgment* to the best of my ability. If I found that I was in the grip of negative thinking, I would gently but firmly stop that line of thinking, take a deep breath, and redirect myself to a place of positive thinking. I practiced this technique for several weeks. And as I'm generally an optimistic, upbeat person, I was astonished at how frequently I found myself caught up in negative thinking.

Then one day, the watch went off just as I stopped at a stoplight…and all at once, the months of practicing my thought-stopping technique culminated in the birth of Stop Breathe Believe. I had experience in stopping my negative thought and taking a deep breath to "reset" my thinking toward the positive. But the missing piece was the Believe component: I needed to replace the single negative thought with a healthy response of my own choosing. I wanted to be more intentional about *choosing* my thoughts instead of having my thoughts manage me. The metaphor of the stoplight was perfect: I'd *stop* negative thinking; *slow down* with a deep, cleansing breath; and *go* forward with a healthy belief statement that replaced my negative thought.

I lean hard into my faith during times of struggle, and I discovered that Stop Breathe Believe was the perfect complement to my practice of prayer and reflection. It enabled me to manage the thoughts in a more mindful way during that difficult time of hard decisions and discerning the best path forward. The practice has been useful in guiding my awareness by helping me look closely at my thoughts, feelings and behaviors. I still use

Stop Breathe Believe often to carry me through difficult situations, and to help me maintain consistency between my deepest, truest self and the decisions that I make.

In this book you'll encounter stories from my own life and from people of all lifestyles and backgrounds who experienced struggles and heartaches on every point of the spectrum. You'll see how they applied Stop Breathe Believe to their unique situations, and you'll learn how you can apply it to your own struggles, large or small.

For many people, the simplicity of Stop Breathe Believe is exactly what appeals to them and the reason it works so well. "When the bottom fell out of the market and the entire firm was in crisis mode," said a corporate manager, "the last thing I needed was seven rules or fifteen steps to remember. What I needed was a reliable go-to tool that got me to work every day and helped me deal with the pressure." The technique is so straightforward that some of my clients have taught it to their families, including children as young as five. Other clients use Stop Breathe Believe as a long-range tool that helps them heal from deep wounds, buried thoughts, and suppressed emotions. A client who came to me for help in working through her early childhood trauma incorporated Stop Breathe Believe into a daily meditation practice. "It's my lifeline," she said. "I didn't think something so simple could have such a profound effect, but it does. I've now practiced Stop Breathe Believe so much that it's just become a part of me."

I encourage my clients to use Stop Breathe Believe in whatever way is best for them, and they've been wonderfully creative in devising new metaphors, symbols, and works of art to aid them in their practice. It's my privilege to share some of their brilliant ideas with you.

A large painting of a stoplight symbolizing Stop Breathe Believe hangs prominently in my office. One of my clients is a talented pianist who suffers from panic disorder and performance anxiety. After just a few weeks of using Stop Breathe Believe, which included belief statements to help her deal with stage fright, she showed up for a session with tears in her eyes. "*This* is what helped me," she said, pointing at the painting. "It's not a miracle...but almost." What a beautiful testimony from a woman who had been grappling with fearful thoughts even the previous week, and who had come very close to missing the musical performance of a lifetime.

Stop Breathe Believe can help you become healthier in your thinking, more intentional in your thoughts and behaviors, more aware of your feelings, and thus more mindful of the beauty of the present moment. It really *can* be a better world.

I can't wait to hear your stories of how Stop Breathe Believe has helped you. Please keep me posted at www.diannemorrisjones.com.

Dianne Morris Jones, LMHC, CDWF-C

CONTROL
YOUR
THOUGHTS?
IMAGINE
IF YOU
COULD!

Elizabeth Gilbert

1

What's On Your Clothesline?

Let's begin with a truism: People come to therapy or turn to self-improvement books because they need help. Whether they're fed up with an obstacle they've struggled with for years, or they're overwhelmed by an unexpected event, or they're suffering from past hurts that call out for healing, or they simply want a companion on their journey for personal growth, people seek help because they've reached a point where they don't want to go it alone.

If you've picked up this book because you've realized you need some help along the way, I applaud your courage in reaching out, and I welcome you with open arms. Stop Breathe Believe has helped bring healing and wholeness to so many people with such a diverse array of struggles that it's now an indispensable part of my therapeutic practice. I'm grateful to the many brave clients who have taught me so much and whose stories fill these pages.

Before I move into showing you how to practice the technique, it will be helpful to know the presuppositions on which my therapeutic work and Stop Breathe Believe are based.

1. My overarching goal as a therapist and as a workshop leader is to *help people grow into wholehearted living.* As terms like "wholehearted" and "holistic" have been used to describe everything from diets to vacation packages to parenting techniques, they can lose some of their force. But they mean just what they say: it requires your *whole*

heart, your *entire* being, to live in a way that honors who you truly are and that brings your unique gifts into being. Lasting positive transformation always occurs on a holistic or whole-person level. Thus I take the whole person into account—the emotional, physical, spiritual, financial, intellectual, and relational perspectives of each person. Wholehearted people live out of a deep, abiding sense of love and worthiness even in the midst of life's inevitable tough times. My goal in this book is to help facilitate your growth into wholehearted living. More specifically, I work from a mindful, cognitive-behavioral-based approach. Traditional cognitive therapy teaches us how to change our behavior by changing our thinking. While this is a valid approach and one I use in my practice, research in neuroscience demonstrates that you can also change your thinking by changing your behavior. What we think affects how we feel, how we feel affects what we do, and what we do affects how we think. Our thoughts, emotions, and actions are inextricably related. I try to bring a mindfulness perspective to everything I do, including the practice of therapy: to be fully aware of the present moment, with the intention of openness and acceptance, and without judgment. If you can picture a triangle with the three points of thoughts, feelings, and behavior, mindfulness is like a sheer curtain over it all that softens the impact of any experience. With mindfulness in place, we can realize that anger, for example, is a feeling that will pass: *I am experiencing a moment of anger*, rather than *I am angry*.

Stop Breathe Believe grows directly out of my therapeutic approach. It offers a unique combination of *cognitive-behavioral therapy, mindful breath-work*, and *the power of wholehearted intention*. It works on the level of our whole being: intellect (thoughts), emotions (feelings), and

THOUGHTS

MINDFULNESS

BEHAVIOR   FEELINGS

[Handwritten margin notes: "Holistic I get — but this def'nition of wholehearted — am I changing for I change my values?"]

[Handwritten notes at bottom: "# what I appreciate = evidence-based ⊕ values, faith, the personal"]

actions (behaviors). I offer Stop Breathe Believe to all of my clients because it works, it's adaptable to even the most complicated life situations, and because it's simple and easily learned.

In this first chapter I'm going to give you a brief description of the overall process so you'll have a quick snapshot of each component and how each works together. The great thing is you do not have to have a complex understanding of Stop Breathe Believe to begin: You can start small after reading this brief description. Benefits can be gained from practicing even one of the parts of Stop Breathe Believe, but it works best when all three parts are integrated and practiced for an extended period of time. Still, nearly all of my clients report improvement after a short time of trying out Stop Breathe Believe. With every succeeding chapter, we'll go a little deeper and see how clients have used Stop Breathe Believe to achieve revolutionary transformation into wholehearted living.

THE STEADY PROCESSION OF THOUGHTS

Picture, for a moment, a comical image: a clothesline attached to both your temples and stretching out into the distance on either side. Pinned to that clothesline is a series of 3 x 5 index cards, each one representing a

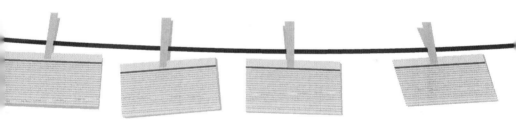

single thought. That line of cards extends as far as your mind's eye can see. The image offers an evocative representation of the countless thoughts that make their way into our brains on any given day. I'm sure you've heard the expression "That went in one ear and right out the other." Most of our thoughts are just like that: They flicker into our consciousness for a moment, only to be replaced by yet another thought, and another. (And who's to say how many unconscious thoughts we have or what's going on at the level of the subconscious?[1]) Some of those conscious thoughts stick around for a while and we find ourselves dwelling on something, and in states of elevated stress we may feel that our thoughts are racing or running away from us. Most of the time, however, we're only marginally aware of most of the thousands of thoughts that enter our brains every day.

But even if we're unaware of those thoughts, they exert an influence on us. That influence can be positive or negative, and when we begin to *act* on our thoughts, those influences make themselves known to our family, our friends, our coworkers—and ourselves. Remember our triangle diagram of thoughts, feelings, and emotions? Well it's simple enough to sketch that out on the page, but in *real* life, with its stresses and complications and characters, things can feel more like a bunch of tangled Christmas lights! We can use Stop Breathe Believe to start untangling one knot at a time.

Love this image! Exactly

Let's say you've got a big exam coming up and even though you studied, you're worried about how you'll do. So far, no problem—you'd be in the minority if you *didn't* worry about your performance on the exam. But that worry gives way to the pernicious thought of *I'm going to fail*. It doesn't matter that you're prepared—the next 3x5 card has already made its way in, followed by the next and the next: *I'll go blank, I won't remember any of the material, and I'll bomb the test.* And if you're like a lot of people, that procession of thoughts is just starting to gather steam. *If I fail, then I won't graduate, and everyone will be disappointed, and I'll never be able to get the job I really want and live the life I desire, and I'll be miserable . . . forever!*

When those rushing 3x5 cards are out of control and you're in the grip of negative thinking, even though you may "know better" and even though all available evidence suggests otherwise, you simply cannot see your way to the truth of the situation. This is how negative thinking works. One negative thought begets another, which begets another, and so on and so forth, every subsequent thought gathering force. Before you know it you're caught up in a wave of pessimism that colors your whole world bleak.

But *somewhere* in the midst of that whirlwind of self-defeating thoughts is a still point of truth—a certainty of what you know deep down to be true. The reality is that you studied for the test, and in all likelihood you'll pass with flying colors. But that one negative thought—*I'm going to fail*—is powerful enough that it can trigger a Category 5 storm. Those negative thoughts begin to swirl and gather strength as they multiply, growing bigger and more powerful, until they can completely obscure the truth. When you find yourself trapped in this kind of unhealthy thinking, you've got to work your way through the inner, self-defeating chatter and find your way back to the tiny, but powerful, still point of truth that is always present.

And that's exactly what Stop Breathe Believe can help you do.

THE GOOD NEWS OF NEUROPLASTICITY

Most of us hardly even acknowledge the deluge of information that floods our brains hour upon hour, minute upon minute—doing so would put us into sensory overload. But neither can we live *mindlessly*, without giving heed to what's entering and influencing our thoughts, emotions, and behaviors.

Exciting developments in the field of neuroscience have demonstrated that what we *do* can change how and what we *think*. And this change even occurs physiologically on a cellular level. Sophisticated brain-imaging technology has revealed that behavior can form new neural pathways in the brain. What's more, it can occur at any point in life. Our brains' ability to form new neural connections in response to experience is called "neuroplasticity."[2] The brain is far more "plastic," i.e. changeable, than has been assumed for decades. This is great news for all of us, suggesting that we have far more influence over things we'd like to change about ourselves than we may have assumed. As Daniel Siegel puts it in his wonderful book *Mindsight*, "one of the key practical lessons of modern neuroscience is that the power to direct our attention has within it the power to shape our brain's firing patterns, as well as the power to shape the architecture of the brain itself."[3] Stop and consider how amazing that is—and how powerful. We can actually change the very structure of our brains through what we do, which includes what we choose to think.

Stop Breathe Believe is based on this premise. One thought at a time, one neural pathway at a time, we can draw closer to becoming the people we want to be. It doesn't happen overnight, of course. But if we cultivate a regular practice, Stop Breathe Believe can help change even long-entrenched patterns of unhealthy thinking. The fact is—and here is a truth statement that surprises many of my clients—*we do have the power to choose what enters our minds*.

Some of you may already be protesting, and with good reason. If you're living at the mercy of racing thoughts, or you can't escape the tyranny of years of pessimism, or you're ruminating on a particular situation or memory, your skepticism is understandable. But I have good news for you, and I can't state it emphatically enough: You *can* learn to choose your thoughts. Whoever you are, whatever your story, you already have within you the power to control what comes in on that endless clothesline. My hope is that Stop Breathe Believe will be a tool that will help you first become aware of your thoughts, and then harness the power to allow in only the thoughts that help you on the journey to wholehearted living, while gently, without judgment, turning away the thoughts that impede you.

Stop Breathe Believe, like any new skill, takes practice, but you *will* get better at it, and the more adept you are at implementing it as a practice in your daily life, the more effective it is. With healthy patterns of thinking, you get healthy patterns of being.

THE FIRST STEPS ON THE JOURNEY

So right now, let's learn the basics of Stop Breathe Believe. My advice is to read this section through once, then another time more slowly, taking notes or highlighting as you need to, and then try the technique out for yourself. I'm going to start with a very general, bare-bones description of the process, and then each time we circle back and learn how different people applied Stop Breathe Believe to different situations, we'll go a little deeper.

Stop: At a predetermined cue (like a stoplight) *or* at a moment you find yourself struggling, *stop* what you're doing and become aware of what you're thinking. You may even want to say the words aloud, using your name: "*Stop*, Brenda;" or "*Stop*, Stephen." Speak to yourself with kindness but firmness. Now, notice what's going on in your mind. Whatever thought you find—and believe me, it could be anything!—simply become aware of it. Just recognize it, and note it without judgment. In keeping with the stoplight metaphor, you'll see throughout the book that I use "negative thought" and "red thought" interchangeably, as well as "belief statement" and "green thought." If your thought is a green, life-affirming thought, take a moment to be grateful! If it's a "red" or life-draining thought, move on to Breathe.

Breathe: As you're able, change your physical position. If your legs are crossed, uncross them and put your feet flat on the floor. Sit up straight so as to be able to make use of your lungs' maximum capacity. Now, breathe in slowly through the nose for a count of four, and then at the top of the breath, exhale through the mouth for a count of eight. The numbers will vary depending on your lung capacity, but the objective is to breathe slowly and deeply, from the diaphragm. You should feel your belly expand with each inhalation. Deep, diaphragmatic breathing triggers the parasympathetic nervous system to relax the body—your heart rate slows, your respiratory rate slows, your muscles loosen.[4] With each exhalation, you'll feel your mind and your body begin to relax. Even if it's for just a moment, *you're redirecting your attention away from the negative thought* you noticed during Stop. You can rest in the Breathe portion of Stop Breathe Believe as long as you like.

Believe: When you feel ready, start to create a belief statement that truthfully addresses the thought you observed during Stop. It may take a few tries to land on just the right one, with just the right tone. In this initial session with Stop Breathe Believe, keep your belief statement short and simple. Let's say that the thought you became aware of was "I'm such an idiot for losing my temper." An effective belief statement could be: "I'm so human." Or: "I'm learning a new process that will help." Or: "Anger does not define who I am." Whatever your belief statement, it's the anchor to get you through the next obstacle. You can use your belief statement in the midst of a tense situation, or as an anchor throughout the day. Other clients choose to tie their belief statement to their breathing, internalizing it with every breath. For example, inhale: Anger does not define me; exhale: I'm learning a new process that will help.

Let's review. Through the process of Stop Breathe Believe you're going to **stop** the endless stream of thoughts and become aware of *one* thought that needs replacing, **breathe** your way to a state of calm openness, and then **believe** a unique truth statement of your own choosing that brings release from the unhealthy thought that's hindering you. Let's now look at each component of Stop Breathe Believe in more detail, and see how some of my clients have used Stop Breathe Believe.

STOP

The first step of Stop Breathe Believe is all about awareness. The vast majority of those 3 x 5 index cards on the clothesline enter our minds without our slightest conscious awareness. So what you're going to do is **stop** your regular activity and your thought process for a moment and simply *notice* what you're thinking. It doesn't matter if you're in the grips of an anxious situation or relaxing comfortably with a cup of tea. The point is to get in the habit of becoming aware of your thoughts. You're learning to cultivate awareness.

Pausing at a stoplight is an excellent way to begin practicing the discipline of Stop, but there are any number of cues you can use. One client practices Stop any time she washes her hands. Another has a screen saver of a stoplight on her computer, and when it pops up she pauses to become aware of her thoughts. Yet another, a client with panic disorder, says he "hits the Stop button" every time he feels tension beginning to rise. It has helped people learning Stop Breathe Believe to have a card in their pocket or screen saver or phone background that features a picture of a stoplight—when they see the reminder, they practice the discipline of Stop. Whatever your cue, once you get in the habit of noticing your thoughts, you'll find that they could be literally anything:

- Did I lock the back door?
- Why did I do that *again*?
- This checkout line is taking forever!
- How many more days until payday?
- I can't *believe* I said that.

Or maybe you find yourself caught up in an elaborate fantasy, or nursing an old grudge, or swept away on a strong tide of emotion—gratitude, love, anxiety, sadness, anger. Most of our thoughts are just idle notions and fleeting images, the byproduct of our extremely powerful, complex brains that are never at rest.

Even fantasies or superficial thoughts can be revealing, especially if you begin to stop and "collect" your thoughts on a regular basis and notice the *patterns* that emerge. Some of my clients keep a sticky note pad in their cars and quickly jot down the thought they "caught" while sitting at the stoplight. Others keep a notepad by their computer, and record their thought when the screen saver pops up. Others post a red piece of paper on the refrigerator and compile a list of thoughts there. Still others have made Stop Breathe Believe a part of a daily meditation practice, and they journal about the patterns of thinking they've observed over a period of time. Especially for those who struggle with runaway thoughts, obsessions, and compulsions, practicing just the Stop part of Stop Breathe Believe is a revolutionary accomplishment that brings great healing and a sense of empowerment.

The Power of Stopping: Brenda's Story

Brenda, a 43-year-old bank executive, had a serious problem with compulsive shopping. By the time she came to my office she was renting a storage facility to house her purchases, and she was close to maxing out her eighth credit card. Her husband was threatening to divorce her if she didn't get help.

Brenda's intake assessment revealed that she was a lifelong overachiever. She'd done extremely well in school and steadily made her way up the corporate ladder; when she she started therapy she was in a high-level, demanding position and was putting in over 50 hours a week at the bank. Although her own finances were in a shambles, she taught a class on personal finance through the local adult education center. She felt her life had started to become "out of control" a year and a half prior when her mother passed away. In the months just after her mother's death she'd "come through just fine," but after the shock wore off and the numerous arrangements and estate details were taken care of, Brenda fell into a deep depression. She took a leave of absence from her job, and it was during those very dark days that she bought an expensive pair of boots to cheer herself up.

It worked. Brenda felt a glimmer of hope—"a little jolt to my system," is how she described it—and she discovered that the more she bought, the better she felt. She could count on "a little jolt" every time she clicked "Buy" or handed her card over to make a purchase. Studies have shown that even *considering* a purchase causes a biochemical change that produces a mental high. "There's a spike of dopamine in the brain at the excitement of immediate form of reward," writes David Krueger in *The Secret Language of Money.* "It makes bad decision-making easy."[5] Brenda even credited her shopping with "dissipating" her grief and getting her back to work. In fact, even though she acknowledged that her shopping was compulsive and that she'd been financially reckless, she had no desire to give it up. And really, it was no wonder. Brenda's shopping was a thoroughly reliable crutch. In a sense, it *had* gotten her back to work. But the shopping was now out of control and threatening her marriage, and it had interrupted the normal grieving process. It was also wrecking her finances. On her most compulsive days she was buying dozens of items and spending thousands of dollars.

Brenda and I began working with Stop Breathe Believe at our very first session, and she decided to tape an image of a stoplight to her one remaining credit card and one to her debit card. This was a very visceral "stoplight" for Brenda that would cue her to become aware of her thinking in the moments before she made a purchase. Her assignment was to *stop* and catch her thought, and then write it down as soon as possible. She affixed a third image of a stoplight to her laptop. This was to get her to pause before making online purchases. Any time she found herself clicking through online outlets, she was to stop, take her hands off the keyboard, and become aware of what she was thinking.

Notice that Brenda's sole assignment at this point was to stop and notice her thinking. I didn't ask her to stop shopping or even form a goal to *eventually* stop shopping. Demanding or asking Brenda to drop what had been a reliable and effective crutch before she was ready would be counterproductive in gaining her trust. And my strong hunch was that there were powerful emotions—specifically, grief—that were driving her purchases. When Brenda had collected enough thoughts, I hoped we'd be able to identify a consistent pattern, and then armed with this new insight into herself, she'd be ready to begin letting go of her emotional attachment to shopping.

But to my surprise, at her third appointment Brenda had some incredible news to share. She reported that at first, she'd found the practice of stopping and catching her thoughts "incredibly unnerving." Why? Because when it came to her online shopping, a good quarter of the time *she didn't even remember landing on the website.* This was mindless living at its extreme; Brenda was operating on autopilot. "Dianne, it was like my hands knew what to do but *I* didn't," she said. "I would go online to check my email, and then it was like I'd wake up and realize I was on the Nordstrom's site." Quite rightly, she concluded that she had "zoned out" for a while. But what Brenda said next impressed me even more.

"What I realized was that underneath the surface thought of whatever I might buy, there was *always* another thought. I'll admit that sometimes I avoided going deep with what I was thinking and just clicked Buy, but every time I took the time to look, the triggering thoughts were always there."

"And can you tell me some examples of those deeper thoughts?" I asked.

Immediately, Brenda began to weep. "Well, they were about my mom. Just totally *random* stuff—not even about her funeral or her final days in the hospital or anything you'd expect. I'd get a memory of her picking me up from school, or letting me pick out a piece of candy at the grocery store, or of me sitting in a pew while she sang in the choir and I wished she could sit with me. I don't even know where all this came from. Half the time it was stuff I'd forgotten about entirely until right then."

Brenda went on to tell me that all of these memories were painful, and that the shopping was a *great* way to mask the pain. As Brenda progressed with the discipline of Stop, she began to take note of how she felt in the minutes before making a purchase. She bought a tiny spiral notebook that she kept in her purse to record her thoughts. She described "a sort of itchy restlessness," and acquiring something new soothed that itch. But beneath that surface feeling of restlessness was a deep well of grief. She started journaling about her thoughts and feelings, and identified the underlying dominant feeling as "a great ocean of sadness." This was very hard work, and Brenda actually felt worse for a time as she began to feel and work through the grief she'd deferred.

Still, within the first month of practicing Stop, her buying slowed. "The stoplight on my bank card helped a lot," she said. "It reminded me of the commitment I'd made to pay attention to my thoughts and my motives." There's a neurochemical reason for Brenda's decreased shopping, too. In *The Secret Language of Money*, Krueger points out that inserting a delay between deciding to buy something and actually purchasing it is an effective way to "help disconnect the dopamine release" that accompanies making a purchase.[6] By intentionally pausing, Brenda was interrupting the cause-effect relationship between a stimulus and the effect it has on the brain's pleasure centers. With that pause in place, she could make a clearer decision. Kruger counsels that we should "take as much time as needed to be able to clearly decide whether the buy makes sense or if you genuinely need it."[7]

With awareness in place, I encouraged Brenda to begin practicing Breathe with more consistency, and if she felt comfortable, to start looking for a belief statement she could hold onto. With Breathe, Brenda made a key insight on her own that took her shopping activity down yet another notch.

"I did what you said and changed my physical position," she said, "and for me it was very important to take my hands off the keyboard. Otherwise I'd just keep clicking. But the physical cue really made me stop, and then I'd turn my whole body away from the computer, close my eyes, and focus on breathing deeply and slowly. The belief statement I'm starting with is *I'm learning to be aware.*"

Brenda was making remarkable progress. I was in awe of the insight she'd gained in just a brief time—and that on her own initiative she was changing her destructive behavior.

That didn't mean, however, that the hard work was done. Brenda had to continue experiencing and living through the grief she'd kept at bay, she had to take concrete steps to get out of the financial quagmire she'd created, she had some repair work to do with her marriage—and yes, ultimately, she had to stop shopping compulsively. She had, in other words, a lot of work ahead of her, and we both knew it would take some time. Brenda continued weekly counseling for just over two years, and she continued to practice Stop Breathe Believe at deeper levels.

"The realization that I was shopping to squash down thoughts of my mother was so powerful—and so humbling," Brenda reported. "Just making that connection let me see that I really didn't need all that *stuff*. I use that word deliberately: I was stuffing myself numb with stuff. Stopping to see what was at the root of my shopping actually helped me to stop shopping. I followed through with Breathe. Instead of avoiding thoughts of my mom—who I *still* miss very much—I decided I'd send her a little hello with my breath. I believe her spirit is alive, and I connect the spirit with the breath. So in a weird way, it gave me a chance to connect with her. I used several belief statements over the course of therapy, but the one I landed on that helped the most was *I am learning to let go of my mom.* It was *so* painful, and I still hurt from missing her, but from early on I knew letting go of my mom was the root of the problem so I decided to tackle it head-on. My husband and I did some great couples counseling, but we both credit Stop Breathe Believe as a tool that helped our marriage and supported me through the worst of my grief. I still use Stop Breathe Believe when I hit a rough patch—when I really miss Mom, when I'm stressed from work, and definitely when I get the urge to buy something I don't need. Stop Breathe Believe is always there, always accessible, and whenever I stop and do an inventory of my thoughts, I always find a revealing insight."

BREATHE

Breathing—giving yourself deep, restorative, calming breaths—is truly the "slow down" portion of Stop Breathe Believe. It's the yellow caution light that signals you to pause to regain your bearings before getting the green light and moving forward. Attention to the breath, or what is sometimes referred to as "breath-work," is an essential practice in so many forms of meditation, yoga, spiritual practice, and relaxation techniques because breathing is so essential to life itself. That may seem an obvious point until you stop to think about how often most of us take our breath for granted. As a function of the autonomic nervous system, respiration is an involuntary process—we don't have to remember to do it or think about doing it. But this life-giving and extremely powerful activity is going on all the time, sustaining us moment by moment.

Gratitude

My belief is that every breath we take, no matter if we notice it or not, is a sacred gift. A deep, life-giving breath precedes the first cry we make when we're born, and our last breath is the consummate herald of our lives on earth. It's a gift all the way, from beginning to end. Viewed like this, every time you notice your breath you're acknowledging a gift—you're bringing a moment of gratitude into your daily existence.

Physiologically, a deep breath that comes from the diaphragm *automatically* brings relaxation to the mind and the body. In fact, if you begin to take slow, deep breaths, you have no choice but to become more relaxed. This is a reliable consolation for anyone who experiences anxiety anywhere on the spectrum, from full-blown panic disorder to the normal jitters we'd get before a presentation or a first date or a big game. That's so important that it's worth stating again: No matter how anxious you are, *paying attention to your breathing and giving yourself the gift of deep, calming breaths automatically triggers relaxation of the mind and the body.* It can eradicate or at least lessen many of the unpleasant symptoms we associate with heightened anxiety: dizziness or lightheadedness brought on by shallow breathing; shakiness; rapid heart rate; excessive sweating; queasiness or nausea; lack of focus or concentration. Deep, intentional breathing has even been shown to be an effective pain reliever. One of my clients refers to his breathing practice as his "windshield wipers for the mind;" another told me just a few deep breaths can "reorient" her mood and give her "a booster shot of energy."

Focusing on the breath and giving yourself the gift of diaphragmatic breathing is one of the best ways to redirect your attention away from troubling thoughts and to bring a state of calm to the mind and the body.

One Breath at a Time: Stephen's Story

Stephen came to see me when he was in his late 40s, well into a successful career in law. He was a partner at his firm and a leader in his community, and had a happy life at home. The area in which he needed help? Managing his anxiety.

Stephen's panic attacks had begun rather suddenly in his mid-thirties, and he attributed their onset to a work event that he experienced as traumatic. Stephen was one of those guys who excelled at everything he did. Driven and keenly intelligent, he was an honors student throughout undergrad and law school as well as a college athlete, and he'd been hired at a prestigious firm straight out of law school. He worked at that firm for more than a decade, rising through the ranks and making a name for himself. Like everyone, Stephen assumed he'd make partner. But as time went on, it became increasingly apparent that it wasn't going to happen. "It was a small city that couldn't support a large firm," he explained, "and it just became a numbers game. I got caught in it." This was the first time that any of Stephen's endeavors hadn't met with success, and it shook him deeply.

Realizing he wasn't going to advance any further, he began searching for a similar position at another firm. One weekend he and his wife went away for what was supposed to be a relaxing getaway. It was then that Stephen had his first panic attack.

"Neither of us had any idea what was happening," he said, still visibly uncomfortable recalling the event from 15 years ago. "Suzanne thought I was having a heart attack and drove me to the hospital. I assumed it was a heart attack too, but what was most terrifying was this feeling—this utter certainty—that something unspeakably horrible was about to happen. I can't even begin to put it into words…just a horrible, terrible darkness and hopelessness, and a certainty that the worst thing imaginable was seconds away. It felt like I was dying and losing my mind all at once. I'd rather have twenty heart attacks than experience one minute of that feeling again."

An ER doctor determined that Stephen was in excellent health, and sent him home with Xanax and instructions to follow up with his regular physician. The Xanax helped, but Stephen now lived "in mortal fear" of having another experience like the one that had sent him to the hospital. He cut the trip short, and saw his regular physician as soon as he could. When his doctor asked him if he'd experienced "a sense of impending doom," Stephen said he nearly jumped off the examining table. "Yes!" He said. "That's it—that's it *exactly*!" It was that day that Stephen learned about panic attacks for the first time, and realized that all the symptoms he'd experienced—chest tightness and pain, shortness of breath, dizziness, nausea, and that awful sense of impending doom—were textbook indicators of a panic attack.

Unfortunately for Stephen there was no quick remedy, and his dread of having another panic attack haunted him. His doctor prescribed Zoloft, but cautioned that it would take 4-6 weeks to have an effect. "I could have cried when he told me that," Stephen said. "Four to six weeks felt like a lifetime." In the meantime, Stephen found himself "petrified" of having an attack in the middle of a meeting or while meeting with a client. On his worst days, his anxiety level was so high that he couldn't bring himself to go into work.

Stephen began weekly therapy with a local counselor, and also began meeting with a group of close friends in whom he confided his troubles. "My friends had no idea what I was talking about," he said, "but they listened and offered empathy, which helped." Stephen said it was through the combination of help he'd sought out for himself—counseling, confiding in trusted friends, medication, and the support of his family—that he made it through "several utterly hellish months." As the medication began to take effect and Stephen explored the causes of his anxiety in therapy, the attacks began to decrease, but he was still haunted by the fear and dread of having another one. This is the familiar anticipatory anxiety that plagues so many anxiety sufferers.

Several months after his panic attacks began, Stephen accepted a position at a new firm, and he and his family moved. By this time he was having no more than one or two panic attacks a year, and he made partner within a couple of years. But his general anxiety level remained elevated, and he still harbored the fear that a panic attack could strike out of the blue, and thus he got back into therapy. That's when I met Stephen.

I taught him Stop Breathe Believe right away, and he began practicing it on a daily basis. Stephen has now been using it consistently for over five years. I asked him to describe what the actual practice looks like for him, and here's what he wrote:

"Any time I start to feel a little funny (when I know my anxiety level is starting to rise, in other words), I do Stop Breathe Believe. It doesn't matter if I'm at work, or at home in bed, at a restaurant, or on an airplane—it works wherever. At times when I'm alone, I'll say 'STOP!' out loud to myself. I say it loudly, and it can pause, if not stop, the spiral of worries that are getting out of control. If I'm in public, I just pause and say silently to myself, *Stop, Stephen.* But I always follow it up immediately with the breathing. For me, the Breathe part of Stop Breathe Believe is the most important. The deep breathing is what calms me down and brings my anxiety level down to a manageable level. I do it for however long I need to. Sometimes, if I'm feeling just a little off, I'll do three or four really deep, slow breaths. But other times it takes 15 or 20, or even 30. Because it's worked so well for me for so long, I have total confidence in the process, and the breathing never fails to bring me relief. Stop Breathe Believe isn't a cure—it seems like I'll always have issues with anxiety—but it is a reliable tool for dealing with the abnormal level of anxiety that will pop up for me from time to time.

"As for the belief statements, I do use those, especially when my anxiety has come up in response to something specific. For example, one time I made an embarrassing mistake at work. I felt awful about it, and for a couple of weeks afterward my anxiety was definitely at an abnormal level. In that case my belief statement was *This one mistake isn't going to ruin your career.* Another time, we didn't get a client we really wanted, and before my anxiety even cropped up I started giving myself a couple of belief statements: *You've got plenty of clients. There will always be other prospects.* I just guide myself back to that truth.

"But again, the most effective part of Stop Breathe Believe for me is Breathe. All the parts work together—I have to stop my spiraling thoughts even to get myself to a place where I can breathe deeply, and I need that truth statement to hang onto going forward—but the deep breathing directly and immediately counteracts my anxiety. That's what I love about Stop Breathe Believe and why it's worked so well for me."

BELIEVE

The believe component of Stop Breathe Believe is where real and lasting transformation can occur.

The first thing to know about "Believe" is that it does not necessarily imply religious belief. (In fact, one client who is a staunch atheist prefers the term "relief statement.") Certainly, if faith is a source of strength and wisdom for you, then your spirituality will inform and define your belief statements. This "green light" step in Stop Breathe Believe is all about whatever you believe in fully and find trustworthy. What's so empowering about Believe is that *you* choose the belief statement that encourages and helps move you toward wholehearted living. I can give you some guidelines, but in the end it must be something from your *own* heart that uniquely addresses your particular situation.

So, what's needed for an effective belief statement? One great place to start is –ing verbs. Runn*ing*, writ*ing*, learn*ing*, think*ing*, read*ing*. These are verbs that are in the process of doing something. It's that *ongoing action* that makes the difference in a belief statement. Belief statements in the form of ongoing action connote a continuing process; they grasp the truth that we are *always on the way* to becoming our best selves. For some clients, –ing verb statements are simply more credible as a first step to transformation than a declaration that implies, "I've arrived; I've got no more work to do." When working with a client early on in teaching Stop Breathe Believe, I encouraged her to believe that she was a strong and confident woman. She looked at me and said, "I can't—I just don't believe that." I immediately self-corrected. "How about *I am becoming a strong, independent young woman*," I said.

Here's a list of many different types of belief statements clients have used:

• I am learning to reach out and ask for help when I need it.
• We all experience shame.
• I am developing a new kind of strength.
• I am learning to manage my stress in a new and different way.
• I am learning to believe that I am important.
• I believe that God has a plan for me, even though I can't see it right now.
• I have a voice and an opinion and I am learning that it is okay to share my truth.

It's with the Believe component of the Stop Breathe Believe process that we begin to come full-circle and are able to change our patterns of unhealthy

It's not just changing the thought = invalidating

thinking. Remember, we accomplish this great work by changing *one* negative thought at a time. So if you've tried Stop Breathe Believe, recall the negative thought you "caught" when you did Stop. It's now time to devise a belief statement that directly addresses that single negative thought. Note that I did not say that the belief statement must "cure" the negative thought or alleviate it or even negate it. In the beginning, we're understanding our patterns of thinking, one thought at a time. We're moving toward healthy thinking one step at a time, one thought at a time, and you're not going to overhaul a long-entrenched pattern of unhealthy thinking with one belief statement, no matter how perfect it is. So here are some examples of very common negative self-talk statements coupled with belief statements that my clients have used.

I'm not worthy.	I believe that I am important.
I am less than.	I am actively becoming the me I'm meant to be.
I feel weak, ineffectual.	I am learning to recognize and use my unique talents.
I'm afraid of not measuring up.	All the evidence indicates I'm doing a great job at work.

Let's look at how Stop Breathe Believe—and a series of powerful belief statements—carried one client through a painful situation at work.

Belief in the Face of Adversity: Janelle's Story

Janelle, a 25-year-old elementary school teacher, loved her job and was good at it. Bright and enthusiastic, she'd been hired right out of college and had excellent performance evaluations. But one day she found herself in a situation with no clear protocol, and she made a split-second decision that had an unexpected outcome.

Two kindergarteners got into an argument, and Janelle intervened. The boys were good friends, and they were arguing over "a toy that they weren't even supposed to have," Janelle said. As was customary, she took the toy and told the owner it would be returned to him at the end of the school day. Then, knowing that the boys frequently played together after school, she asked them to apologize to each other. One boy did so, but the other refused. Janelle reminded him that they were friends, and that friends should be kind to each other. Still he refused, and by now the rest of the class was getting restless and Janelle was losing patience. She told the boys that they'd have to stay inside at recess until they both apologized. They made up, but the one who'd been forced to apologize later complained to his parents, and the parents filed a grievance against Janelle. They felt Janelle's intervention had crossed a line, and that their son shouldn't be forced to issue an insincere apology.

No matter where you come down on the issue, the result for Janelle was that she was given a verbal reprimand and written up—and the experience was profoundly disturbing. "I had a black mark on my permanent record!" she said, only half joking. To make matters worse, she'd thought she was doing the right thing, and it felt as if the school administrators had turned on her. "I totally understand that writing me up was just school policy," she said, "but I really wish they'd had my back more in the meeting with the parents. I've done good work there consistently, and it was like all that was forgotten when I made one stupid misstep."

At first, Janelle was angry and hurt by how she'd been treated by the administrators, but then she couldn't let it go. And as she tended to be conflict averse she didn't go to the administration, but dwelt on her complaints internally. Soon it was all she could think about, and though she had a good track record, she started to feel like a failure and an ineffective teacher. Janelle expected to feel a reprieve from her negative thoughts during the summer, but in fact her worries increased. It got so bad that she gave serious consideration to resigning, and it was only with monumental effort that she went back to school in the fall. Her husband couldn't understand why she couldn't just let it go, and why she couldn't stop thinking about it. As Janelle became increasingly distressed, he encouraged her to try therapy. "I just can't get out from under this thing by myself," Janelle said at our first meeting. "It's spiraled out of control."

With Janelle's use of Stop Breathe Believe, the process was to navigate our way through the storm of negative thinking that had blown out of control, and work our way back to the truth that lay obscured by her outsized reactions. In brief, the escalation in her unhealthy thinking went like this:

> I made a careless mistake → My one stupid mistake is now in my permanent record → After years of teaching I should have known better → If I can get this one thing wrong, I can get anything wrong → Maybe I'm really not an effective teacher after all → I'll probably get fired over this → I should probably just go ahead and quit → I'm a failure as a teacher → I'm a failure.

Laid out in such stark terms, it's easy to see where Janelle's thinking went awry. But when you're in the midst of the storm, you can't see past the self-defeating thoughts that have you in their grip. And that's where Janelle was. A competent, effective teacher who enjoyed her job, she was now "a nervous wreck," constantly worried that her colleagues were monitoring her and looking out to "nail" her on her next misstep. "I'm at the point where this has completely hijacked my ability to teach," she said. "And I've taken the stress home, too."

Janelle's cue was to practice Stop Breathe Believe at the beginning and end of her lesson planning. Janelle chose this cue because she wanted something specifically connected with her job, and because it would require her to do Stop Breathe Believe frequently. She placed an image of a Stop Breathe Believe stoplight on her desk as a reminder (see Appendix IV on page 187 for examples). Not surprisingly, the majority of the thoughts she "caught" during Stop were self-defeating statements about her job and her abilities. She made a list of them, and was taken aback to realize how dark her thoughts had become. "My beliefs about myself have turned toxic," she rightly pointed out.

To directly counteract her "toxic" thinking about herself, Janelle was going to have to come up with some strong belief statements. She got help from daily readings from Melody Beattie's *The Language of Letting Go*, a book about letting ourselves feel all of our emotions, accepting powerlessness, and owning our own power. Notice how Janelle's belief statements move from simple to increasingly complex.

1. It's helpful for me to talk about this.
2. I am so human.
3. I am learning from my mistakes.
4. I am not defined by my mistakes.
5. I am realizing that I made one misjudgment among a multitude of right decisions.
6. I'm learning to give words to my insecurity after making an isolated mistake.
7. I'm ready to let go of this.

While *I'm ready to let go of this* may seem a simple belief statement on the surface, it was actually the last step in Janelle's progression to healthy thinking. She wasn't ready to let go until she'd claimed the truth of the six preceding belief statements.

Over the course of her year in weekly therapy Janelle regained her confidence, and she still uses Stop Breathe Believe on an as needed basis. "Any time I'm in a situation where I have to make a major decision or a quick judgment I use Stop Breathe Believe," she said. "In the latter case when it's a spur-of-the-moment thing, I'm only able to stop, take one deep breath, and then come back to the belief statement *I now trust myself to make the right decision*. But it gets me through. That's the value of having a belief statement already in place—it's there, I know it's the truth, and I can depend on it. Any time I feel a little wobbly, I go back to that belief statement, and it carries me. I learned to love my job again, and I got my confidence back."

BELIEF STATEMENTS TO HELP YOU GET STARTED

1. I am learning a new process that will help.
2. It's okay for me to tend to my own needs. ◀——
3. I'm learning to accept my inherent worth.
4. I'm learning the truth that I am more than my feelings.
5. I don't have to know everything before trying something new.
6. I am learning to let go.
7. It will be liberating to become aware of only one thought at a time. ◀——
8. I'm choosing to accept that asking for help is a strength.
9. I'm growing into showing up and claiming my life.

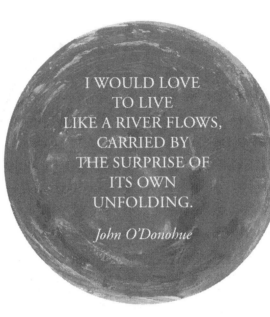

I WOULD LOVE
TO LIVE
LIKE A RIVER FLOWS,
CARRIED BY
THE SURPRISE OF
ITS OWN
UNFOLDING.

John O'Donohue

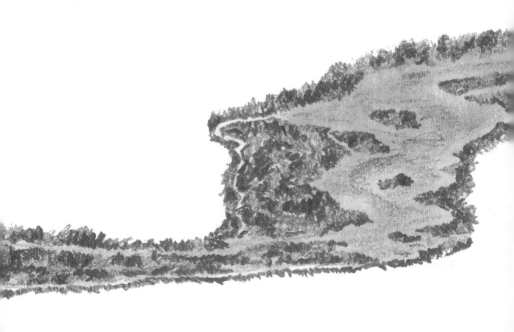

2

Ruts and Rivers

It's been said that the journey of a thousand miles begins with one step. Whether it's a literal journey you're taking or an inner journey to wholeness, you'll arrive at your destination by taking one step at a time. This is true of Stop Breathe Believe as you learn the process. Like any new skill it will take a little getting used to and some practice to get the hang of it. But used regularly, Stop Breathe Believe is a powerful aid in becoming aware of and then redirecting the negative thinking that impedes our journey to wholehearted living.

There's another sense in which that "one step at a time" mindset applies to Stop Breathe Believe. If you find yourself worrying that your challenges run so deep that they've got the best of you, or that it just doesn't seem possible to find your way to a place of lasting relief, let me offer you a comforting thought. Your job isn't to overhaul a lifetime's worth of unhealthy thinking in 30 days or six weeks. It's to use Stop Breathe Believe as a tool in helping you move consistently into the new territory of wholehearted living *one thought at a time*. That's all you've got to do: Take that one step, address and redirect a single negative thought.

Picture a powerful river, deep and wide, with a swiftly flowing current. Yet even the mightiest river can be diverted by a relatively small alteration to its flow. The change occurs one stream of water at a time, as one small rivulet leaves the old path the river has followed for years and breaks off into new territory.

It's not about never having bad thoughts again. When they come up, how do we address them?

We can all come up with examples of negative thinking that are so habitual they've now cut a deep "riverbed" into our minds. They've been with us so long and are so ingrained in our thinking that they've taken on the veneer of truth. *I'm going to be single forever. I'll never lose weight. Someone else will always get the promotion. They'll think I'm stupid.* Thoughts like these can become so second nature to us that we don't even stop to question their validity or their objective reality. And really, it's no wonder. These deep "riverbed thoughts" have forged neural pathways in our brains; in a sense we're wired to think the way we do.

But as we saw from the last chapter, we do have the power to change and heal from deeply embedded negative thinking. Just as we hold the power to "wire our brains," we hold the power to *rewire* our neural pathways to enable patterns of thinking that better serve us. Daniel Smith, in his memoir on anxiety *Monkey Mind*, writes about the moment he realized that he held the power to change deeply embedded unhealthy thought patterns:

> I didn't yet realize that a quarter century of anxiety has gouged deep, packed-earth ruts in my brain, and that the only way to stop my thoughts from falling back onto those ruts was to dig new tracks and keep digging them, forever. I didn't yet realize that the only nonnegotiable approach to the anxious life is discipline.[8]

A turning point for Smith arrived when he realized that it was possible to deal with his chronic, debilitating anxiety through disciplined action, through a consistent forging of new neural pathways. Simply put, he could change his thinking through his actions—and therefore live without anxiety overrunning his life.

Redirecting one thought at a time gets easier with each new thought you address—you can get in the groove of *forming* new grooves! It just takes a commitment to redirecting one thought at a time, and doing so consistently. That's how you'll accomplish that journey of a thousand miles to your own deep place of truth and trust.

JACKIE: A STEADY EROSION OF BOUNDARIES

Jackie, 32 and single, came to see me for help with a problem at work: her lack of boundaries. At first glance this may not seem like an emergency problem or a deep riverbed of unhealthy thinking, but for Jackie it had reached those levels. During our first session she candidly said, "My job is killing me. I'm ready to quit just to stay sane." We may have heard that comment from a friend or coworker, and possibly even said it to ourselves.

Jackie was the office manager at a very busy law firm. Not only did she keep things operating smoothly for the executive employees, she supervised the office staff, coordinated operations between international offices, and oversaw the interns. She was putting in more than 60 hours a week. Her job hadn't begun this way, but her responsibilities had steadily increased over the years until she was doing the work of two or sometimes even three people. She told me she was "sick to death of it," and that it wasn't fair that she had to do it all.

After I learned some more particulars about Jackie and her incredible workload, I asked what her thoughts were on what was keeping her from changing the situation.

She looked at me incredulously. "Well, who *else* is going to get the job done?" she said. "There's no one else who can do what I do, not even close! There's no time to train someone else, and worse, there's zero backup system. If I go, that place is going *down*."

"And what are *you* getting out of this arrangement?" I asked.

Jackie thought about that for a moment. "Well, they do compensate me well," she said, "so there's no problem there. And everyone, from the senior partners on down, tells me they couldn't get along without me, and they thank me for my work."

As we continued to talk, Jackie admitted that she relied on the affirmation and approval the positive feedback gave her. The reality is that she was right: The office really couldn't run without her, and that gave her a sense of power and importance. Her self-esteem soared especially in times of crisis, when she could swoop in and save the day. It was hugely self-affirming to be the hero and to be so needed, and it was great to get the recognition she deserved. But Jackie also recognized that even with these positives in place, the overwork made her feel stressed, taken advantage of, and resentful.

"I don't have any boundaries, Dianne," she said. "I know this about myself and I see the damage that's happening because I've become such a people-pleaser, but I don't know what to do about it or how to change it. This has been going on for *years*."

In subsequent sessions Jackie and I talked about the deeper reasons for her desire to please others, and we explored the "riverbed" issues that were silently encouraging her to allow herself to be taken advantage of. With the practice of Stop Breathe Believe, I especially wanted her to capture the negative thoughts that were most present in her mind—the repeat offenders that had her stuck in a rut. Jackie began keeping a notepad by her computer, and when she found herself starting to feel resentful or stressed out, she stopped and jotted down what she was thinking. Then she gave herself what she called "a mini break" by taking a deep, rejuvenating breath. One deep breath was about all she felt she had time for in the middle of her hectic workday, but it was a good start and a huge improvement in an environment that kept her adrenaline constantly revved.

After a few weeks of catching and recording her thoughts, Jackie came in with a Top Four she'd culled down from more than a dozen:

Red Thoughts: Jackie's Repeat Offenders

- I have to do it all.
- It isn't fair that I have so much more to do than everybody else.
- There is no backup system of help for me.
- I'm pissed off because the partners aren't willing to train or hire anybody else.

Now, in Jackie's case, before we could begin creating belief statements that would open a path to genuine transformation, we had to discuss her role in *creating the conditions* that were making her miserable. Jackie needed to realize that her craving for affirmation and approval was, in effect, causing her to hoard all the work. She was doing this unconsciously, but by ensuring that she alone was knowledgeable enough to get the job done, she ensured that she garnered the approval she craved. A huge part of her identity and self-esteem was based upon her work performance. When she received praise, she felt great. But when no praise arrived, she felt unappreciated or even implicitly criticized.

And in setting herself up to be the sole person in the office able to carry out the duties of two or even three people, she had set herself up for an incredible amount of stress, and as we were now seeing, deep resentments. She needed to learn to set boundaries, and to delegate.

Over the next months, we worked to establish the crucial self-awareness that would allow Jackie to begin re-framing her tendency to base her identity and self-esteem on the accolades she received for going above and beyond the call of duty at work. Clearly, before she could begin addressing the thought and behavior patterns that weren't serving her well, she had to become aware of them, and of their negative effects on her. This is where Stop came in. As she was going through this awareness process, she began seeking out moments in the workday when she could give herself a "mini break" and take some deep, calming breaths. Her next step was to create some effective belief statements to begin redirecting one negative thought at a time, and to create an actionable plan to get some relief at work.

Here are the "red" thoughts Jackie caught with Stop, followed by the "green thoughts" (or belief statements) she used to address them:

Red: I have to do it all.
Green: I am learning to establish boundaries.

Red: It isn't fair that I have so much more to do than everybody else.
Green: I choose to begin to create the conditions for a fair workload.

Red: There is no backup system or help for me.
Green: I am learning to delegate and train others.

Red: I'm pissed off because the partners aren't willing to train or hire anybody else.
Green: I am willing to let my anger go and apply my energy to asking for help.

One of Jackie's concrete goals to get some relief was to take a lunch break away from the office. She was accustomed to eating at her desk and working through lunch, barely aware of what she was wolfing down. During her time away she would use a half hour to do nothing but eat, followed by a half hour to practice Stop Breathe Believe. Her absence from her desk also signaled to her coworkers—and most importantly, herself—that she was creating a firm boundary and had a life apart from work that was worth tending to.

"I clung to those belief statements, but I also really enjoyed the Breathe part," Jackie said. "The office is such a beehive I knew I couldn't concentrate on just sitting still and breathing if I'd stayed there, so it was nice to get away and clear my head. It left me more serene, and more ready to deal with whatever stresses were waiting for me in the afternoon."

The real breakthrough for Jackie came in noticing the patterns inherent in her red, or unhealthy, thoughts—the repetitive patterns that after so many years, had become those deeply ingrained "riverbed thoughts."

"I realized I had a *slew* of red thoughts," she said. "And when I caught a bunch of them and wrote them down, there it all was, plain as day. *Life's not fair. Everyone dumps on me. Everybody expects me to do it all. The office would crumble without me. I'm worn out and pissed off. There's no one who can help me.* I had this moment where I was like—Whoa, is this really me? Is this who I've become? And it was! It happened little by little, but I had become a miserable, resentful person. Everyone *did* dump on me because, without actually saying it, I'd allowed them to—for years! Now I see that I made sure I was the only one who could do x, y, and z, because then I'd get the recognition for it. I let my job description blow up, one little task at a time, until I couldn't take it any more."

The next part of Jackie's actionable plan was to go to her supervisor and tell him she needed help. Because she'd built so much of her identity around being able to do it all, asking for help was a big challenge for Jackie—she resisted it because it felt like admitting defeat. Many people feel this way, and assume that asking for help is a sign of weakness. But it's actually a *huge* strength. It takes a great deal of honest awareness to realize that we need help, and a great deal of courage to ask for it. I often advise clients to write this belief statement down prior to an important meeting or a critical conversation: *Asking for help is a strength.* Jackie did ask for help, and to her surprise the firm agreed to hire an assistant.

"Seeing how stuck I was in negative thinking was a real wake-up call," Jackie said. "When I had all those thoughts down on paper, I saw the slippery slope I'd fallen down. I'd let one boundary slide after another, and now I'm putting them back in place. So that was the first thing Stop Breathe Believe did for me—just gave me some self-awareness. After I became aware of my negative thinking, I knew that implementing change was up to me, and I really liked that. I excel at assignments, and I liked the sense of empowerment. And I did it! I followed through and made the changes at work that made my life better. I actually like going to work again."

We never consciously choose to become stressed out or miserable, at work or anywhere else. It happens over time, after a steady accumulation of days and a steady accumulation of choices that don't support who we are at our core and how we want to live. But if we're not happy at our jobs—where many of us spend most of our time—how will we be happy elsewhere?

Six months after beginning therapy, Jackie reported feeling "relaxed *and* empowered." She now visits with me every other month for a check-in, and we continue to explore the deeper issues that sometimes drive her need for approval from outside sources. Her job is still very high-energy. Incorporating Stop Breathe Believe into her life has helped her to feel she's on top of things rather than always trying to put out fires. "I can't believe I waited so long to ask for help, and to give myself some down time," she said. The practice of Stop Breathe Believe is now a part of her lunchtime routine, and she's planning to teach it during the next intern training program.

DWIGHT: TAPPING INTO A RESERVOIR OF MOTIVATION

When I met Dwight he was 42 years old and morbidly obese. He was under the care of a doctor and a nutritionist, but he'd made little progress in sticking with a wellness program, and he'd stalled out completely when it came to exercising. He was pursuing counseling because he wanted help with motivation, with regard to exercise especially.

My heart immediately went out to Dwight. *All* of us know how difficult it can be to lose weight or get that workout in. There are a million good reasons why we don't have time for exercise or why it can wait. But for Dwight, it couldn't. He got winded walking from his desk to the break room, his blood pressure was high, and he was on the cusp of developing diabetes.

Adding exercise to his life was going to be an uphill battle. Dwight weighed over 370 pounds, and his lifestyle was almost completely sedentary. When I asked him what his fitness goals were, he said, "Well, my ultimate goal is to weigh 200 pounds or less."

That would require Dwight to lose nearly half of his current body weight. "That's a great long-term goal," I said, "but what about before that?"

"I'd like to get my health back."

"Also a perfect long-term goal!" I said. "How about a few steps before that?"

"I want my blood pressure to be in a normal range," he said. "And for all of this stuff to happen, I know I need to exercise."

"Okay," I said, "let's concentrate on the exercise, and let's back up a few steps. Let's think for a minute about what it would take to get you out of your house and through the gym doors."

"Okay, so like, smaller goals."

"Exactly," I said. "One step at a time. Smaller, more manageable goals, goals you can build success on one step after another."

I grabbed a legal pad and quickly sketched an image of a lake with small feeder streams here and there. "The main part of the lake represents your brain," I said, "and these little streams are all the various thoughts that make their way in. Some of these thoughts are unproductive and unhealthy, and it's those we want to divert." I drew in a rock that cut off a negative thought stream. "And maybe there's another stream way over here that we want to redirect into our river—our brain," I said, and drew a stream off to the side. "With intention, awareness, and practice, we can divert that stream to our larger river. So let's bring our attention to some thoughts and practices that can get you to the gym. One step at a time."

Dwight sighed and studied the ceiling. "Well," he finally said, "I guess it would depend on a lot of factors. I work 8 to 5 and I'm not a morning person, so going to the gym would have to happen at night. And there are certain nights that are out—I've got stuff to do on Wednesdays, Fridays, and Sundays."

"Okay," I said, "that leaves four more. What would it take?"

Again Dwight studied the ceiling. "Honestly, it would depend on how I feel…you know, if I had the energy and was up for it and all. You know?"

I did know. I have a long list of excuses that bump exercise down the list. Even when I know I should exercise, even when I want to, there are times I choose to do something else. Many of us know this feeling.

As Dwight and I got to know each other better, I realized how deep his aversion to exercise was. He didn't even like to use the word "exercise." So one of the first things we did was identify a more positive expression, something that wouldn't turn Dwight off immediately. Our goal then became to *increase his movement*. This also worked because it was a far more easily accomplished goal than an expression Dwight found intimidating like "working out" or "hitting the gym."

I asked Dwight to use Stop Breathe Believe to catch his negative thoughts about movement. Here are the red thoughts he came up with:

Red Thoughts: Dwight's Repeat Offenders

- I don't have enough time for exercise.
- I could be doing something else.
- I'll start tomorrow.
- People at the gym are going to stare or laugh at me.

Dwight had a lot of self-awareness, and I commended him on it and his willingness to admit some hard truths about himself. With Dwight, we had two immediate objectives. One was to get him moving, even a little bit, and the other was to start shifting his thoughts about exercise and movement, *one thought at a time*. These two objectives would positively reinforce each other. Any increase in movement would show him that he really could do it. And changing his thinking about exercise would make it far easier to actually *do* the exercise. As he began to let go of some of these old thoughts, he could develop a new perspective, a new way of seeing himself.

Knowing that we needed to set Dwight up with small goals so he could achieve some quick success and gain confidence, we came up with three movement goals.

1. During TV commercials, he was to walk to the kitchen and drink some water (no soda!).

2. He was to take the stairs to his second-floor apartment rather than the elevator.

3. Right after waking he was to do arm lifts—the movements you'd do if you were doing stationary jumping jacks. He'd start with ten reps, and add more once he felt stronger.

To many of us these seem like easily attainable objectives, but for Dwight they represented stretch goals. He was going from almost zero movement to three new ways to add movement to his life on a daily basis. And the second goal—taking the stairs—was going to be physically challenging for him.

Meanwhile, Dwight set to work on coming up with green statements to counteract his deep-rooted negative thinking about exercise. His first set of green statements provides an interesting and instructive example because without intending to, Dwight formed counterproductive belief statements. This is not unusual when unhealthy thinking is deeply embedded.

One at a time, let's take a look at four sets of his original red/green statements, and then I'll show you why they weren't working for Dwight and how together we created empowering belief statements that would support his exercise goals.

Counterproductive Belief Statement #1
Red Thought: I don't have enough time for exercise.
Green Thought: I DO have time for exercise.

"Dwight," I said, "you're right that you do actually have time to exercise, but has telling yourself that ever worked for you in the past?" He admitted it had not. "Well then, let's see if we can come up with something that will help get you moving and not criticizing yourself for past behaviors," I said. "Just your being here shows me that you're at a new point."

After some discussion, we decided to base his new and improved belief statement upon an opportunity for increased movement that Dwight had already built into his routine. Remembering the value of starting small, the new belief statement would support *one* specific movement goal. Dwight revised his first red thought/green thought pair.

> *Effective Belief Statement #1*
> **Red Thought**: I don't have time for exercise.
> **Green Thought**: I'm going to start small and go to the kitchen for a glass of water during commercials.

Next Dwight shared his red thought/green thought combination about what he'd rather be doing than exercising:

> *Counterproductive Belief Statement #2*
> **Red Thought**: I could be doing something else.
> **Green Thought**: If I want to live, I don't have any choice but to exercise.

It was perfectly true that Dwight's health depended on his willingness to make healthy choices, including adding exercise to his routine. But "I don't have any choice" included an element of unwilling coercion, a loss of autonomy and self-empowerment. It was also too condemnatory a statement; Dwight stood a very good chance of sooner or later rebelling against his own belief statement or giving up, overwhelmed. Condemning statements are not motivating, even to ourselves, or maybe *especially* to ourselves.

"Okay, how about this," Dwight said. "Red thought: I could be doing something else. Green thought: More movement will help me do the things I *really* want to do."

"Bingo," I said.

We followed up with making a list of things that Dwight really wanted to do, and used those specifics in his belief statements.

> *Effective Belief Statement #2*
> **Red Thought**: I could be doing something else.
> **Green Thought**: More movement will help me get to Gray's Lake, walk to the bridge and back, and eventually, walk all the way around.

Dwight's third belief statement concerned general motivation:

> *Counterproductive Belief Statement #3*
> **Red Thought**: I will start tomorrow.
> **Green Thought**: I WANT to start today.

I affirmed Dwight's desire to begin an exercise program sooner rather than later, but I thought a little more specificity would help. Dwight came up with a knockout on his first revision:

Effective Belief Statement #3
Red Thought: I will start tomorrow.
Green Thought: The earlier I start, the better off I'll be.

The last belief statement we worked on together was the most troubling.

Counterproductive Belief Statement #4
Red Thought: People at the gym will stare at me or laugh at me.
Green Thought: If people stare or laugh it will give me greater motivation to lose weight.

Dwight's fear of being ridiculed at the gym was legitimate, and to his credit he had good intentions in trying to turn this fear on its head and use it to his benefit. But this belief statement—*If people stare or laugh it will give me greater motivation to lose weight*—was shame-based, and shame is not a good motivator. Never has been, never will be. At best, it can inspire only temporary motivation, and it's a shallow motivation at that—at some point, shaming yourself into pursuing a goal *will* backfire. It's based upon self-criticism, and eventually you'll become resentful and distrustful of this very destructive motivator. World-renowned sociologist and shame researcher Dr. Brené Brown says it best: "Shame corrodes the very part of us that believes we can change and do better."[9]

Shame is insidious, and it can pop up where and when we least expect it. Without knowing it, Dwight had come up with a belief statement that actually *undermined* his motivation to lose weight and regain his health. And in his particular case, if he failed in his goals I knew he'd stand a very good chance of returning to his trusted companion and comforter, food. I also feared that the dread of being stared at or laughed at would overpower Dwight's desire to go to the gym. So it was especially important that this belief statement was effective.

As clients are finding their way out of the realm of their own deep riverbeds of negative thinking, I ask them to think of what a loved one would say to them. This can be a friend, a spouse or partner, a sibling, a parent—anyone you trust and whom you know has your best interests in mind. That's just what I did with Dwight. I knew he had an excellent relationship with his doctor, so I asked him to imagine how his doctor would encourage Dwight to get to the gym. Ultimately we can't rely on others for our motivation, but getting Dwight to step into his doctor's shoes for a moment was a good first step in getting him out of his shame-based point of view.

"Well, what he always tells me is that I deserve to be healthy," Dwight said. "That I owe it to myself to get my health back."

"With that in mind, what do you think your doctor would say to you?"

Based upon Dwight's answer, together we came up with a more intentional belief statement that incorporated the idea of giving himself the gift of health and that reminded him of his self-worth.

Effective Belief Statement #4
Red Thought: People at the gym will stare at me or laugh at me.
Green Thought: I value myself enough to commit to making healthy choices.

"And Dwight," I said, "there's another gift I want you to give yourself."

"What's that?"

I smiled at him. "Do you own a pair of running shoes?"

It's so important to take these big goals one step at a time, and for Dwight, shoes were a good place to start. He went to the local running store and got fitted for a great pair of shoes—which in itself was an act of courage for him. It took courage to go in among all those seasoned athletes and ask for help, and it was also a great practice for entering the gym.

Then at the gym, Dwight was in for an encouraging surprise. There he encountered people at all levels of fitness, and he found himself inspired by some of the other beginners who were struggling but still maintaining a commitment to their health. He also joined a class that was specifically designed for overweight people. The instructor, he learned, had once weighed over 400 pounds. "That was really cool," Dwight said, "to hear—and *see*—a success story like that."

Dwight's progress was remarkable. It took such courage to go to the gym and be vulnerable, and to risk the chance that others might stare at him or even make fun of him. The reality turned out to be that no one made fun of him, and though he did notice a few sidelong glances, he was now able to entertain an alternative viewpoint.

"It's entirely possible," he said, "that they're looking at me the way I look at the other heavy people at the gym. As an inspiration."

At the time of this writing, Dwight has lost 64 pounds. He uses the stairs regularly, and he goes to the gym three times a week. When he finds himself tempted to skip a workout, he pictures the other people from his class and remembers their commitment. "We all rely on each other," he said. "If somebody misses, they can expect to get a text or a call."

He also ended up further revising his first green statement. Originally it had been about starting small and going to the kitchen for water during commercials. "Now I've upgraded it, Dianne," he said. "My new green statement is 'I can always find a chance for more movement.'" Dwight found that he enjoyed the challenge of finding little moments in the day in which he could add more movement. "It's kind of like a game," he said. "Where can I find even a minute to put in a little more? I do those arm lifts first thing and right before bed now, too. At work I only use the bathroom farthest from my desk so I can get in more steps. I always take the stairs. Sometimes when I'm watching TV I do arm lifts. Or even smaller things—like when I'm waiting for the coffee, I rise up and down on my toes. Anything to burn a few more calories."

I could not be any prouder of Dwight! It took a lot of inner resources and commitment for him to join a gym and follow through with going regularly.

But my level of pride doesn't even approach Dwight's. "I can't believe I'm doing it!" he said. "I'm really doing it. The last place I ever thought I'd be was on a treadmill. My new goal is to work up to a slow jog by spring. And in the summer—I'm doing Gray's Lake, even if it takes me three hours to get around it."

OLD MOVES, NEW GROOVES

Jackie and Dwight both experienced serious challenges that stemmed from deep-rooted patterns of negative thinking. Jackie had been doing the lion's share of work at her office and unconsciously *ensuring* that was the case—for so long she no longer knew any other way to do her job. Dwight had such an aversion to exercise that he no longer considered the possibility that he could learn to like it or even tolerate it—not even when his life was quite literally in danger.

When you're stuck in a rut this deep, you can no longer discern the truth from the falsehoods that unhealthy thinking is feeding you. Jackie just accepted that there was no other way to do her job or to conduct herself at work. Dwight assumed that he "wasn't an exercise person" and that he'd always be dangerously obese.

With complex challenges like Jackie's and Dwight's, a host of therapeutic practices and new tools are necessary. In counseling, Jackie explored why she was so driven to seek approval from outside sources, and began learning how to be content with the approval she could find within herself.

Dwight worked with a physician and a nutritionist and his exercise class to help him lose weight, and he and I explored some of the reasons he was overeating and how to begin building a new and healthy relationship with food. Both Jackie and Dwight added Stop Breathe Believe to their toolboxes in order to reveal the *patterns* of unhealthy thinking that were preventing them from living wholeheartedly. Once those patterns were revealed, it was a great relief to know that their task wasn't to dismantle the entire pattern of unhealthy thinking that had been inhibiting their journey to health and happiness. Their job was to address and redirect *one* negative thought at a time with a healthy belief statement. That's all. One thought at a time. Even that can feel like a lot, and it can take a lot of courage.

Remember our river example? If we assume our job is to divert the Nile we've already set ourselves up for failure. But we absolutely *can* begin to shift one small stream, and then another, and another. *Our brains are wired to do this.* The longer we stick with new behaviors and new thinking, the stronger the neural pathways that develop.

Flowing water that's confined to one path etches a progressively deeper groove into the earth. Given enough time, it can create a groove as deep as the Grand Canyon. But as vast as the Grand Canyon is, it's no match for the power of the human brain, and the strength of human motivation. You already have within you the power to change years of negative thinking to positive, healthy thinking. Commit to redirecting that one thought at a time, that one thin rivulet of water, and you're well on your way to the path of health, wellness, and wholeness.

BELIEF STATEMENTS TO GET YOU OUT OF THE RUT

1. Wholehearted doesn't mean I have to be perfect.

2. Healthy love means giving AND receiving.

3. My feelings are valuable.

4. I'm learning to accept the present moment without judgment.

5. I'm learning to accept that I don't have to know everything.

6. All shall be well, and all shall be well, and all manner of things shall be well.[10]

7. I'm learning to see the richness in being intentional.

8. There is strength in feeling and expressing my vulnerability.

9. People will still like me even if I disagree.

LIFE DOES NOT
CONSIST MAINLY
—OR EVEN LARGELY—
OF FACTS AND HAPPENINGS.
IT CONSISTS MAINLY
OF THE STORM OF THOUGHTS
THAT ARE FOREVER
BLOWING THROUGH
ONE'S MIND.

Mark Twain

3
Swirling Funnels & Storm Shelters

Kayla is a 22-year-old college junior studying business. She's an honors student with a 3.8 GPA and is in a long-term relationship with her boyfriend Jordan, a software developer.

Kayla came to see me about anxiety. She described herself as being generally nervous and high strung, but it was with the possibility of graduation looming and not knowing what to do next that her anxiety had become unmanageable. We spent our first meeting exploring the history of her anxiety, how she experienced it, and the coping strategies she already had in place. She listed long walks, listening to relaxation podcasts, and talking to Jordan; she described Jordan as her primary form of support. Kayla and I began creating some simple yet powerful green thoughts that she could use immediately to help get relief from anxiety. The simplicity of Stop Breathe Believe is one of the things that makes it so efficacious when you find yourself overwhelmed. Kayla's initial green thoughts were: 1) I'm learning a new technique that will help and 2) Anxiety is a feeling that will pass. At one meeting she told me that she'd taught Stop Breathe Believe to Jordan, and he'd found it so effective in dealing with presentation jitters that he'd taught it to his teammates at work.

Then one day Kayla arrived at her session in tears. Jordan had been recruited by a major tech firm and he was moving to San Francisco. Kayla was sad, of course, but she was terrified about the prospect of a long-distance relationship. She described herself as having racing thoughts, and she couldn't get scenarios of Jordan cheating on her out of her mind. She found herself demanding to know where Jordan was when they weren't together, and had snuck glimpses of his phone to see whom he was texting. "I *know* it's crazy," she said. "I mean, Jordan has never given me any reason to doubt him… but I can't help myself. I'm 99% sure he's not cheating *now*, but who knows what will happen when he gets to San Francisco and starts meeting new girls? Girls who are prettier and curvier than me."

My first step into the storm of fear and jealousy with Kayla was to examine her "racing thoughts" via a funnel diagram I often use with clients. When your thoughts are spiraling out of control and you find yourself caught up in a whirlwind of negativity and fear and pessimism, I call this *the swirling funnel effect*. Picture a dangerous funnel cloud absolutely teeming with negative thoughts and destructive self-talk and self-sabotaging tendencies, all swirling out of control. Or sometimes, the funnel may be teeming with strong emotions whose source we can't identify through all the dark clouds and thunder and wind. In fact, this experience is so common that it inspired the creation of my first book, *I'm Fine*: *A Real Feelings Journal*, which helps you identify and journal about your feelings. Whatever your funnel looks like and feels like, it's incredibly difficult to find your way through that storm to the truth that's way down at the very tip of the funnel, to the place of calm and clarity that will allow you to think and speak freely and authentically. The first step in navigating this storm is to identify the self-defeating thoughts at the top of the funnel. Simply naming those thoughts gives you a greater sense of control, and thus alleviates a measure of anxiety. Then as you're ready, you make your way layer by layer through the funnel, until you arrive at that still, small point of truth.

Several years back, when I was just starting out with Stop Breathe Believe, Roger and I made one of our many trips to Texas for the holidays. We'd been in Iowa for years, and though we'd kept up with Texas friends and family regularly via email and phone, it was wonderful to see everybody in person, and we all had a great time reconnecting. But by the end of the trip I was ready to get back home and to my regular routine, which included the kind of quiet time I need to recharge. So you'd think I'd be nothing but pleased to be returning home after a fun, meaningful trip, but all the way home from Texas I found myself gripey and irritable. For the most part I kept my baffling irritation to myself, but not talking about it and not understanding its source made me even more irritable and frustrated. Which made me even more irritable and frustrated!

My irritation continued into the next day, and soon it was all I could think about—what was going on with me? Was it post-holiday letdown? Was I just overtired? All I could see and feel was the negative emotion and confusion—I was stuck in the top of the swirling funnel. But as soon as I remembered the image of the funnel, I stopped what I was doing and used Stop Breathe Believe to re-center myself. I needed to get through all that inner chatter—the emotions and my confusion about the emotions—to arrive at the point of what was giving that whirlwind energy. After I became deeply relaxed through some slow, deep breathing and calmed myself with the belief statement "By slowing down and paying attention, I'm getting to the diamond of truth, which for me is richer understanding," I sketched out my funnel, going deeper and deeper one thought at a time. It looked like this:

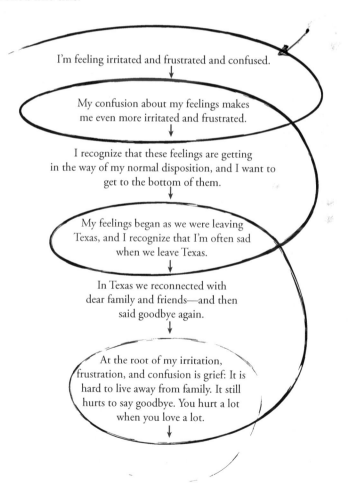

I'm feeling irritated and frustrated and confused.
↓
My confusion about my feelings makes me even more irritated and frustrated.
↓
I recognize that these feelings are getting in the way of my normal disposition, and I want to get to the bottom of them.
↓
My feelings began as we were leaving Texas, and I recognize that I'm often sad when we leave Texas.
↓
In Texas we reconnected with dear family and friends—and then said goodbye again.
↓
At the root of my irritation, frustration, and confusion is grief: It is hard to live away from family. It still hurts to say goodbye. You hurt a lot when you love a lot.
↓

It took me nearly two days of feeling the storm and then *sitting with it* long enough to get through it to arrive at the place of truth. That's how the funnel works: We have to make our way through all the inner chatter and the details of a situation in order to get to the calm, quiet place where the truth is waiting to be found. Sometimes you'll need to talk with a trusted friend or a therapist or sit in solitude or pray to get to the tip of the funnel. Sometimes you can journal about your feelings and find your way to the truth. Sometimes engaging in a physical activity such as walking or cleaning or golfing leads us to an answer by not actively striving for it.

Elizabeth Gilbert, in her memoir *Eat, Pray, Love*, describes the life-changing moment when a fellow seeker informs her that she can cultivate the power to choose her thoughts. At first it seems to her "a nearly impossible task." But according to her friend, choosing thoughts is about "admitting the existence of negative thoughts, understanding where they came from and why they arrived, and then—with great forgiveness and fortitude—dismissing them." Gilbert is convinced she wants to try it, and realizes it will require much time and practice.[11] Here's how she describes the process:

> I repeat this vow about 700 times a day: 'I will not harbor unhealthy thoughts anymore.' Every time a diminishing thought arises, I repeat the vow. *I will not harbor unhealthy thoughts anymore...*A harbor, of course, is a place of refuge, a port of entry...The harbor of my mind is an open bay, the only access to the island of my Self...This island has been through some wars, it is true, but it is now committed to peace, under a new leader (me) who has instituted new policies to protect the place...This is a peaceful harbor, the entryway to a fine and proud island that is only now beginning to cultivate tranquility. If you can abide by these new laws, my dear thoughts, then you are welcome in my mind—otherwise, I shall turn you all back toward the sea from whence you came.[12]

I shared this quote with Kayla, and then after a brief session of Stop Breathe Believe to become centered, Kayla identified some of the "diminishing thoughts" that were causing her so much pain. Here's the funnel diagram we sketched together (FIGURE A).

When we finished, Kayla frowned. "It's good but I'm still not all the way there," she said. "We probably need to do a second funnel for other stuff." And by the way, your funnel can have as many layers as you need; Kayla wanted to start over with a new one focusing on a different subject. Kayla's second funnel captured her thoughts of "not enough" and "what if" (FIGURE B).

FIGURE A.

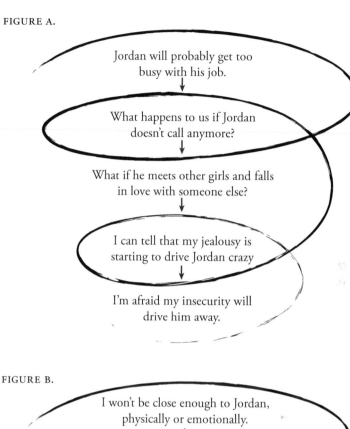

FIGURE B.

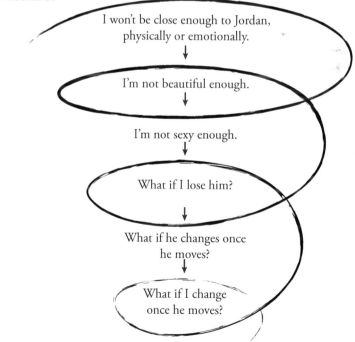

We now had a long list of the negative thoughts that were causing Kayla significant anxiety and hampering her relationship with Jordan. I asked Kayla to talk about her strengths, the things she knew to be true and liked about herself. We'd then build her green thoughts around those core truths. Here's her list:

- I'm caring.
- I love to learn.
- I'm confident.
- I'm loyal.
- I'm organized.
- I'm growing as a person.
- I have a lot of coping skills.

And here are the green thoughts that Kayla came up with regarding Jordan's impending move and her anxiety about being in a long-distance relationship:

- Distance does not erase love.
- My passionate personality will help sustain a long-distance relationship.
- I am learning not to get hijacked by my insecurities.
- I am willing and able to invest in our relationship, whatever the obstacles.

As it turned out, Kayla's suggestion of a second funnel was a brilliant one. Together, we "superimposed" one funnel on top of the other, and saw that at the root of her anxiety about Jordan cheating and moving away was a deep insecurity about her body—and beneath that, about not being good enough. She feared not being "good enough" for a long-term relationship with Jordan—because after all, it *felt like* he was leaving her. When she threw light on her thinking in this way—in other words, when she brought it out from the confines of her mind, where her thoughts were becoming distorted by anxiety—she could see where her thoughts had gone off track and were simply not true.

Kayla then came up with a new list of green thoughts—short, powerful statements that addressed the *root* causes of her distress.

- I am learning to see myself as beautiful.
- I am worthy of love.
- I am worth the wait.

Kayla and I both looked at each other and smiled when she came up with that last one. *I am worth the wait.* It was a perfect green thought for Kayla, and it's a great belief statement generally. I suggested that she say it aloud right then and there. And without prompting, Kayla repeated "I am worth the wait" several times, each time gaining strength and confidence. She'd found shelter from her storm.

GREEN THOUGHTS FOR NAVIGATING THE SWIRLING FUNNEL

1. I CAN find shelter in a storm.

2. I am worthy of shelter from any storm.

3. I can rely on the strengths I know I have.

4. Exploring my swirling funnel will help me understand myself.

5. Truth can be found at the still point of the swirling funnel.

6. Naming the thoughts in my funnel gives me a sense of security.

7. By slowing down and paying attention to my thoughts, I'll reach my safe harbor.

8. I will try not to harbor unhealthy thoughts.

9. Nurturing myself is a safe harbor.

THE SOUL
BECOMES DYED
WITH THE
COLOR OF
ITS THOUGHTS.

Marcus Aurelius

4
Going Green

These days we hear all about the great value and outright necessity of "going green" in order to protect and restore our environment. I'd like to suggest that "going green" in our thinking and in our self-talk is just as urgent if we want to live a life of wholeness and reach our full potential in the world.

We've already seen the great dangers of unhealthy thinking and negative self-talk—allowed to proliferate unchecked, destructive self-talk can sabotage a life. But the practice of cultivating healthy thinking and positive self-talk is life saving. "I feel brand new," said an 87-year-old client whose primary belief statement was *I choose to hold on to hope.* "I've got a whole new life ahead of me." Her experience was one of the clinchers for me in deciding to write this book. If Stop Breathe Believe can inspire a woman in the twilight of her years to see a whole new life ahead of her, that's the final testimony I need that it can help people. Let's look more closely at how Stop Breathe Believe can help us go green in our thinking—and in our living.

THE GREEN BRAIN 101

Healthy living and healthy interactions with others start with healthy thinking—with a brain that's gone green! When "our brains function as an integrated whole," Dr. Daniel Siegel writes in *Mindsight*, "our relationships thrive. But sometimes we 'lose our minds' and act in ways we do not choose."[13] To understand how the green or fully integrated brain

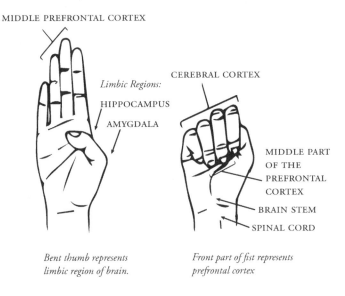

MIDDLE PREFRONTAL CORTEX

Limbic Regions:

HIPPOCAMPUS

AMYGDALA

CEREBRAL CORTEX

MIDDLE PART OF THE PREFRONTAL CORTEX

BRAIN STEM

SPINAL CORD

Bent thumb represents limbic region of brain.

Front part of fist represents prefrontal cortex

works, let's look at Siegel's well-known hand model of the brain.[14] With your own hand, you can see the interconnectivity of three basic regions of the brain—the brainstem, the limbic area, and the cortex—and how disruptions in the prefrontal cortex cause temporary loss of our higher-order thinking abilities and lead to poor interactions with others.

To try it out for yourself, place your thumb in your palm and then curl your fingers down over the thumb. Your wrist now represents your spinal cord, and if you lift your fingers and thumb, you'll see the brainstem area in your palm. Put your thumb back on your palm and you've got the limbic area. Finally, curl your fingers back over your thumb, and you're looking at the cortex.[15]

So, what do these three areas do? The **brainstem** connects the spinal cord to the midbrain, and it controls the major involuntary functions of your body. Your beating heart, your breathing lungs, your blood pressure, and states of arousal such as hunger or sexual desire are all controlled by the brainstem.[16] The **limbic area** is comprised of several different organs and is responsible for creating our emotions. It also plays a crucial role in how we become emotionally attached to one another and helps us create different forms of memory.[17] The **cortex** is the outermost layer of the brain. It controls sophisticated, higher-order functions such as thought, consciousness, language, and perceptual awareness. Finally, if you look at your middle two fingernail areas on your hand model, you've got the middle prefrontal cortex. It's this area that allows us "to pause before we act, have insight and empathy, and enact moral judgments."[18] If you lift your fingers up and put them back down, you'll see that the prefrontal cortex connects *all* of these regions. As Siegel puts it, the middle prefrontal cortex "is literally one synapse away from neurons in the cortex, the limbic area, and the brain stem."[19] And without that middle prefrontal cortex fully engaged and "online," we're not functioning with a green brain. The stage is thus set for reactive temper tantrums, meltdowns, and confrontations.

So what does all this mean for us? Simply this: Going green in our thinking and our living requires a brain that's functioning as an integrated whole. With what we know regarding neuroplasticity, we know that our own choices, activities and thoughts can enhance or diminish our brain regions' capabilities. Stop Breathe Believe can help us choose the activities and thoughts that will best help us go green in our thinking and in our living, and ward off the kind of toxic thinking that isn't doing us—or anyone in our lives—any good.

You may be familiar with the computer-programming acronym GIGO: Garbage In, Garbage Out. If you're allowing or even actively feeding "garbage" into your brain in the form of unhealthy thinking, you will inevitably produce "garbage out" in the form of unhealthy thinking *and* actions. Thoughts affect behavior.

The good news is, *behavior also affects thoughts*—and that's the key to transforming trash into treasure. While Garbage In may produce Garbage Out, positive corollaries are equally true. Choose your own metaphor: Beauty In, Beauty Out. Love In, Love Out. Compassion In, Compassion Out. Serenity In, Serenity Out. It's never too late to change, and with the power of neuroplasticity and the intentional practice of going green in your thinking one thought at a time, there's no negative thought, feeling, or behavior that can't be recycled into something useful and even beautiful. We *all* have instances of "Garbage Out" thinking that need to be transformed. Many people would say that Garbage Out simply needs to be disposed of—let's get rid of the trash! I understand where they're coming from, but my view is that everything, even our worst shortcoming and our most shame-filled mistake, is salvageable when it catalyzes positive change and becomes the raw material of growth and healing. Granted, we can't get stuck with the "trash," but we can make efforts to recycle even what at first glance seems the most valueless parts of ourselves. It's all part of the process of positive transformation, and all worthwhile in the journey to wholehearted living.

GREENER THINKING, GREENER INTERACTIONS

Learning more about "the green brain" made all the difference for my client Lois. Lois came to see me because she was "arguing constantly" with her two sons, ages 14 and 12. She even described her house as a "warzone." Through tears, she admitted that she was having a terrible time with her sons' growing independence. "I *know* they're growing up and they *should* be spending time with their friends," she said, "but I just can't stand it. The more they try and do things on their own, the more I clamp down."

I asked Lois to describe what a typical interaction would look like if, say, one of her sons asked to sleep over at a friend's house.

"I hate to even say," she said. "It's usually a screaming match, at least with Nate. He's always been more confrontational than his big brother... Aaron just stomps off to his room and won't come out. Usually at least one of us ends up crying. But no matter how bad it gets, I can't let them go."

"How about sports or other extracurricular activities?" I asked. "Do they participate in anything?"

Lois looked at the floor and shook her head.

"Has either of the boys given you reason to think that they shouldn't be allowed to do things on their own away from home?" I asked.

"No," she said. "They're good boys. I just want them with me. When you're a single mom you have to do *everything for everybody*," she said. "I run a tight ship and we operate like clockwork at our house. Doing it all by myself is exhausting, and if the boys are with me it's just easier. I don't have to worry that way."

Part of Lois's Garbage In thinking was the assumption that she had to do "everything," when in reality her sons were old enough to take part in household responsibilities and in helping to manage their own

schedules. While she believed she was doing what was best for her family, her controlling methods of micro-managing the schedules and never allowing Aaron and Nate to do things away from home were in place to alleviate her own anxiety. Further, Lois was still recovering from the pain of divorce and grieving the loss of her marriage. So we had a combination of challenges to address, some of which called for immediate relief, and some that we'd deal with over the course of therapy.

I asked Lois what happened if her schedule ever went awry.

"That's exactly why I'm here!" she said. "I can't handle it at all. I flip out. I've said awful things to the boys. I've screamed at them that they must not love me if they're so eager to get away all the time…that they don't have a clue what I'm going through and don't appreciate anything…that they're selfish and ungrateful…And worse. I hate it so much, and they hate it, and I'm so *tired* of screaming. It's bad at our house, Dianne."

Lois's recovery process is complex, multifaceted and ongoing. During her early months of therapy, we worked on her controlling impulse. Lois used Stop Breathe Believe in two primary ways. First, as a useful *preventive* technique. Lois rose fifteen minutes earlier and started each day with slow, deep breathing and the repetition of her green thought—*I am choosing a better way*—as a mantra. Intentionally starting the day in a calm, peaceful manner sent a powerful signal to her brain and her wounded heart that she was doing something different and more life-giving. It helped her to *continue* the day in a calmer, more peaceful manner. One snag Lois ran into was a common experience among most people who are new to meditation or any other mindfulness technique. When she was first trying to bring some inner and outer quiet into her life, her thoughts actually seemed to become *louder*. We discussed this in session, and I assured her that her experience was perfectly normal and that it would take some time for her frenetic "monkey mind" to become accustomed to the quiet. However with continued practice—and Stop Breathe Believe, while easy to implement, does require dedicated practice—the brain learns new pathways, and we're able to draw from the kind of deep, healing silence that informs our thinking and our interactions with others.

Second, as much as she could, she used a "micro-meditation" form of Stop Breathe Believe in the midst of tense, high-stress situations. When she sensed a confrontation brewing with her sons or felt that her anger was beginning to spiral out of control, she used Stop Breathe Believe to check herself. Even if the entire Stop Breathe Believe sequence consisted of stopping for a second or two, taking one deep breath, and remembering *I am choosing a better way*, Lois was learning to respond to her sons in a more thoughtful manner, and she was building new neural pathways associated with responding rather than reacting. She needed an external cue to arrest the toxic thought patterns and the toxic behaviors that arose from them until her brain could learn a greener way of thinking that would inspire greener interactions. Through her intentional efforts to alter her actions, her thoughts were slowly shifting, and her feelings were following suit. The whole tangle of toxic actions, thoughts and feelings were in the process of going green; in time, the pause and the thoughtful response would become second nature.

After weeks of her practice and her new, greener way of being, Lois reported that she was making progress and that there was less overall tension in her home. She'd allowed the boys to join a soccer league, and said she was working up to letting them do overnight trips. But the day that I showed her Siegel's hand model of the brain as shown on page 66, a light bulb clicked on for Lois.

"Oh my gosh I see myself in this *so much!*" she said. "All of those times I was caught up in the moment and yelling and blurting awful things—my brain was pretty much offline. I was just reacting, without even paying attention to what I was thinking."

As Siegel would put it, Lois's pattern had been to move "directly from limbic impulse to speech and action" instead of accessing her prefrontal region, which allows for empathy and higher judgment.[20] This knowledge was especially liberating for Lois because she's a person who loves information, and to have more knowledge helped her feel more in control—but in this case, in a healthy way! She now understood what was happening when those three parts of the brain are un-integrated—and more importantly, that *it was entirely within her power* to "re-wire" her brain to support healthier thinking, and thus, healthier interactions with her family. We revisited our earlier conversation in which she indicated that she would "flip out" and start screaming, which was a clear example of being disconnected from the healthy-response part of her brain. Another passage from *Mindsight* beautifully captures the going-green process Lois was experiencing:

> Response flexibility harnesses the power of the middle prefrontal region to put a temporal space between input and action. This ability to pause before responding is an important part of emotional and social intelligence. It enables us to become fully aware of what is happening—and to restrain our impulses long enough to consider various options for response.[21]

In Lois's case, Stop Breathe Believe served as the intentional pause she needed in order to restrain her impulse to say or do something hurtful. That ability to stop, refocus, and go forward with a thoughtful response rather than a mindless reaction transformed her family dynamic, and it transformed how Lois saw herself.

Lois continues to work on her control issues through therapy and with Stop Breathe Believe, and an anti-anxiety medication has helped as well. Already, there are outward manifestations of Lois's beautiful going-green process. She smiles and laughs more, and Aaron and Nate, now 15 and 13, are attending after-school functions and spending more time with friends. In addition, one unanticipated benefit of having her sons more socially involved is that *Lois* is more socially involved. Before she was isolated; now she's made friends with some of the other parents, and sharing common stories of struggles and triumphs has been healing in itself.

"The boys and I still have our moments," Lois said, "but that's part of being the mother of teenagers. I've learned to be more flexible and let go of little stuff that doesn't really matter. I'm learning to let go in another sense, too—to let go of the boys, at least a little more. Sometimes I literally clench and unclench my hands to remind myself of how bad it feels to be tight and constricted, and then how liberating it feels to be open. Our house is so much more relaxed and fun now."

"No more warzone?" I asked.

"Maybe a few skirmishes here and there," Lois said with a smile. "But no more warzone."

GRADUALLY GOING GREEN

Whereas Lois came to me with specific complaints of control issues and the friction-filled relationship with her sons, Michael, 41, arrived at my office without knowing exactly why. Sheepishly, he mentioned "maybe a midlife crisis." He couldn't pinpoint the source of his general malaise and vague sense of unease. "I can't get it out of my head that there's just got to be something *more*, you know?" he said. "And that's something's just… not right. I don't know how else to put it." He shook his head, frustrated. "I mean, I feel like a jerk for even complaining—I've got a great marriage, two great, healthy kids, my childhood was normal, I make enough money, my friends are solid guys…what have I got to complain about, right?"

"And yet you're here," I said.

"And yet I'm here," he agreed.

The first step was to affirm Michael's feelings. Feelings are just feelings—we're not to judge them or judge ourselves for having them. Feelings come and go, but they're valuable indicators of our inner state, and they're present for a reason. Though Michael couldn't yet put words to his feelings, he did sense, quite correctly, that something was amiss. I asked him if he'd be comfortable doing a simple breath exercise to try and get in touch with deeper parts of himself. With back straight and feet on the floor, he was to place his hand on his belly and take five slow, diaphragmatic breaths. If he were breathing effectively he'd feel his hand on his belly rise. With every inhalation, he was to say (mentally or aloud), *I am making space for my true emotions.* This exercise was pushing at the edge of Michael's comfort zone, but he agreed to try it at home. I gave him a copy of the Feelings List (see Appendix I on page 182) to help him along. This is a tool I've used many times in my practice. The Feelings List helps identify specific nuances of emotion, rather than overarching categories like "sad," "happy," or "mad." It can help clients who live in their heads get in touch with their feelings, it can help people who are overwhelmed with emotion differentiate and specify their feelings, and it can give clients language for inner experience that can be difficult to articulate. After the deep breathing, Michael was to write down any emotions he discovered, and if he needed help, he could turn to the Feelings List.

The next week, Michael returned with this list:

• apprehensive
• ashamed (somewhat)
• bored (a little)
• confused
• curious
• frustrated
• melancholy (slight)
• restless
• uncertain

Besides Michael's qualifications to the feelings (somewhat, a little, slight), one item on his list caught my eye immediately, but we went through each feeling together. The experience of apprehension was no surprise— Michael was a bit anxious about his vague state of distress for which he could attribute no cause. He was somewhat ashamed about being in therapy "when other people have big, emergency problems." He found himself slightly bored with his life though he had no specific complaints, confused as to why he felt the way he did, and frustrated that he couldn't "snap out of it." Discouraged that he couldn't discern a reason for his restlessness and boredom on his own, he was slightly melancholy, and uncertain about what had landed him in therapy and what would make him feel better. All of this was consistent with what Michael had told me during our first meeting.

The one feeling that leapt out at me was curious. This one was different, and I sensed it could provide an entry point for getting to the bottom of Michael's vague dissatisfaction. I asked him to tell me more about why he felt curious.

He blushed. "Well, this may sound crazy, but one way you could look at this whole therapy thing is kind of like a quest, you know? I mean, I've never needed to 'go deep' or whatever because everything has always been *fine*. But now something's different, and I want to figure this thing out. So I'm thinking of therapy as something like a quest…like I'm going on a journey to find answers about myself."

Michael's metaphor of a quest is a beautiful one.[22] I told him that the idea of a quest or a hero's journey is an archetypal theme in many cultures—and that his own intuition had provided him with the exact metaphor he needed at this point in his life. I encouraged him to follow that curiosity and together we'd see what we could find.

One of the impediments to Michael's journey of healing was all the "shoulds" and self-judgments he was placing on himself: I should be able to figure this out on my own; I shouldn't be complaining; I'm ashamed of complaining when there are people with much larger problems than mine.

I so often hear some variation of this very common worry. *What right do I have to complain when atrocities are occurring in the world? My suffering isn't as great as so-and-so's; how can I even think of complaining? I shouldn't feel bad when other people are so much worse off than I am.* Most of us have probably engaged in this "comparative suffering"[23] at some point or another. But other people's suffering, no matter how great or small it looks from the outside, has no bearing on our particular experience. Green thinking acknowledges that we feel what we feel, period, and that those feelings are legitimate and worthy of attention.

Further, when you try and repress those feelings, they'll inevitably emerge in some less than ideal way, and before you know it you're caught in the muck of Garbage In, Garbage Out. I shared with Michael my own experience of comparative suffering; it's a story I often tell clients who fall into the trap of devaluing their experience in comparison to others'.

Several years ago my friend Helen experienced a horrible tragedy when she lost her husband and three sons in a boating accident. Needless to say, I couldn't even begin to fathom what Helen was experiencing. The entire community of Amarillo, Texas was devastated by the accident.

Four years after the accident, my family moved from Texas to Iowa because an amazing career opportunity had come up for Roger. It was July of 2000; Justin was a freshman in high school, Jill was going into seventh grade, and I had just finished my Master's degree in counseling.

Once we moved in to our new home, I became the self-appointed "transition specialist" for everyone. I threw myself into helping Roger and the kids get adjusted. I even deferred job-hunting so I could be available for everyone full-time. The problem was, I forgot about helping *me* get adjusted!

I also ignored my feelings of deep grief about leaving Texas and our friends and family, telling myself that I couldn't fall apart because I had to be the one to make the transition for our family as smooth as possible. And when feelings of sadness or homesickness did start to bubble up, I did the comparison thing. *Well at least you have your kids*, I'd tell myself, remembering Helen. *At least you have your husband.*

So, although I had plenty of big, urgent emotions that were calling out to be felt and dealt with, I steadily pushed them aside by denying or minimizing my own suffering as compared to Helen's. *Buck up*, I told myself. *How can you even waste any time feeling sorry for yourself when your friend lost her husband and her three sons, and your family is fine?* And so on and so forth. The lie of comparative suffering is that it delegitimizes and discourages your own very real, very present feelings, and when those feelings don't get *felt*, much less processed in a healthy way, they come back to haunt you.

Roger started his new job within days of the move, and Justin and Jill started school in August. September was spent getting the house all settled. By the time October rolled around, I was crying all day as soon as everyone left the house. I hid my depression as best I could. When the kids got home from school I pulled myself together and tried to be the wife and mom I thought my family needed. I cooked all the dinners, I cleaned, I helped with the homework, I drove everyone to every practice and play rehearsal and appointment. But the next morning it would begin again and I'd cry and wander around the house in a mental fog.

I thought I was doing a grand job of hiding my true feelings until shortly before Christmas, when Jill pointed to a photograph on the refrigerator of me with my Texas friends. "Mom, I wish you still looked like *that*," she said. "You never smile any more." All at once it dawned on me what had happened. After many weeks of denying my feelings and trying to minimize them by comparing my suffering to Helen's, all that accumulated unfelt sadness had crossed over into depression. I couldn't help but feel a little chagrined—as a trained therapist, I was supposed to know what to do *with* depression, not *be* depressed. As if therapists are immune from depression!

By the time we went back to Texas for the Christmas holidays, I had reached the end of my rope. Roger and I went to see the counselor in Amarillo that I would've worked for had we remained in Texas. Roger asked if we should consider moving back, and said he was willing to quit his job if it was best for our family. We discussed with the counselor the pros and cons of moving back to Texas and decided that what we were going through was a growing experience for us all. A doctor prescribed an antidepressant for me, explaining that my depression was situational and that medication would be like jumper cables that would get me back on track. And he assured me that I *would* get back on track eventually. Our counselor urged Roger and me to make an appointment with a therapist first thing when we returned to Iowa. We did, and through the journey of counseling I felt all those feelings I'd been deferring and devaluing, which was the very means to my recovery.[24]

There's no value whatsoever in denigrating or devaluing your own emotions, whatever they are. Comparative suffering is Garbage In thinking that can be transformed. Yes, atrocities occur in the world every day, and yes, someone's story may sound worse, but your unique experience is still *real* and *true* and *worthy of attention.*

+ gratitude

And this was certainly true for Michael. I explained to him that part of his journey would be to get through all the "noise" of the shoulds and shouldn'ts he was placing on himself and go on a quest for his particular truth.

"I get what you're saying and it all sounds good," he said, "but how do I actually *do* that? How do I get down through all the junk and find out what's really real?"

"You've already started the journey," I reminded him. "You're here, and you're asking the right questions—and is it fair to say that several weeks ago you were struggling with what questions to ask yourself?"

"Absolutely," he said.

"Well every week you're going to take a few more steps on the quest, and there's a tool I'm going to teach you that will help."

That's when I introduced Stop Breathe Believe to Michael. By this time he was more comfortable, and we did a few practice runs in the office. The first green statement he came up with was great: *Every step on the quest takes me closer to me.*

"I was going to say 'takes me closer to truth,'" he explained before I even asked, "but I need it to be more personal. I'm getting to know my true self, so it just seemed to fit."

Michael's cue to launch Stop Breathe Believe was the moment he became aware of those vague feelings of restlessness and dissatisfaction. Usually, this was late at night when all the busyness of the day was done and his mind was unoccupied. His first several attempts to do Stop Breathe Believe were frustrating. "I'm having trouble quieting my mind to do the deep breathing," he said.

I wondered if Michael were actually rushing too quickly past Stop. I suggested he spend more time capturing his thoughts, and to pay special attention to the ones that showed up repeatedly. That exercise revealed a great deal. Soon, Michael brought in this list of Garbage In thoughts:

- You haven't accomplished anything truly significant.
- You're running out of time.
- You're fifteen years into a career that doesn't make a real difference in the world.
- You still don't even know what you *really* want to do with your life.
- Deep down, you know the life you made for yourself isn't enough.
- It's AWFUL of you to feel like such a great life isn't enough.

Notice that all of Michael's unhealthy thoughts were in the second person. His worries about how he was living his life and who he had become were personified in a very critical, accusatory voice that constantly found him wanting, and insisted that he was running out of time. This is classic Garbage In thinking.

"Michael," I said, "before we move into talking about your green statements, I want to ask you a question, and I want you to wait until this two-minute hourglass is completely empty before you answer. Use that time to do your breath practice and try and get down to the truth."

The two-minute hourglass is something I periodically use to build a short period of silence into a session. It's fascinating to see how that tiny amount of time and silence helps people move past knee-jerk or superficial reactions and get to a deeper response. In couples' counseling, it also prevents partners from interrupting each other, which alone helps move past old hurts of feeling disregarded, not valued, and not heard— sometimes literally.

I asked Michael when he felt most like his real self, the true Michael, and then turned over the hourglass.

For the next couple of minutes Michael closed his eyes and breathed deeply. His answers came quickly: playing soccer with his kids; intimate moments with his wife; going on long bike rides; hiking; just relaxing with family and friends.

These were all good, true answers, but my sense was that there were answers even farther down. "Great," I said. "Now let's *start* from this point, and go even deeper. This time, without negating anything you just said, I want you to imagine ways you'd *like* to feel the real Michael. Don't censor yourself—just let your thoughts run wild and take you wherever they want to lead you. What are some things that would energize you, enrich you, lead you to feel the most authentically Michael?" This time I let the two-minute hourglass empty twice.

With eyes still closed, Michael began to talk. "I...I've always wanted to hike the Appalachian Trail," he said. "The whole thing, Georgia to Maine. And I want to travel. I've barely been out of the state, and I'd love to see new places—to take Mindy and the kids to new places. I can even—and this is crazy—I can even see us living overseas for a while, doing some kind of service project. I just want to get plugged into something bigger, way bigger, than my one individual little life. It's a good life, a great life, but I feel in my gut there's *more*." He opened his eyes. "Does that make any sense at all?"

It made perfect sense. There comes a time in most everyone's life—and Michael was at that classic midlife point when it occurs for so many people—when we take that first bracing look at our own mortality, and wonder if the path we've chosen is the most life-sustaining and meaningful one, or if there's more we could be doing beyond our own "individual little lives," as Michael put it. Or as Mary Oliver famously wrote, "Doesn't everything die at last, and too soon?/Tell me, what is it you plan to do/ with your one wild and precious life?"[25] Michael's life was great, but it had come to feel too small. He wanted to widen the scope of his vision to include more than his immediate circle of friends and family and coworkers. He wanted to follow his desires to live bigger, live bolder, and live with intentions directed toward others instead of self.

As we continued to talk Michael's eyes misted over. "I want to be a better role model for my kids," he said. "Not that I'm a negative role model now, but I want to be *more positive*. I want to expose them to different places and different people, and show them how to live generously. I've been given so much, and I want to pay it forward."

Michael's thinking was definitely going green, and now he wanted to find green actions that supported his new, more life-giving mindset.

Because a year in a foreign country or hiking the full Appalachian Trail wasn't feasible for his immediate future, we talked about ways he could begin to follow his desire to live more true to himself in the present moment. (And in the meantime, he began saving and planning for a trip when his children were a bit older.) He kept coming back to the desire to be "plugged into something way bigger." So we came up with a list of service opportunities in his own community that he and his family could become involved in right away. This was a great start, but I also wanted Michael to be able to begin meeting that need for more *that very day*. And for that he needed to become aware of even smaller moments in which he could celebrate the life he was already living, and celebrate his new, more capacious vision. We talked about the practice of consciously choosing to find the beauty and worth in everyday moments and being on the lookout for beauty in unexpected places. This is a powerful green thinking practice, and a great way to train your brain to go green.

He agreed to try it, and even began carrying around a small notepad to jot down his observations. He called these his "binocular moments." As the weeks progressed, all those little observations added up to a whole that made sense to Michael. "It's *all*, even the boring stuff and the stuff that seems to make no sense at all, part of the quest," he said. To put it simply, Michael learned to look at and think about his daily, ordinary life in a new way. Everything he did—his job, taking the kids to soccer practice, the dishes, the errands, the bills, the laundry—could now be seen through the lens of the quest, the hero's journey. His ability to see *all* of his life as part of a greater whole, even the smallest, most mundane details, gave him a sense of being far beyond himself. His life didn't feel so small and isolated any more. That shift in thinking was profoundly transformative.

Michael found a way to go green in his thinking and in his living in the very midst of all the regular details of regular life. He found wonder in the present moment, in reality just as it is. Now that's green thinking and green living at its best.

SOME GREEN THOUGHTS FOR GOING GREEN IN YOUR THINKING

1. I'm learning to let go of self-judgment.

2. Going green in my thinking is an act of love I can give myself.

3. Healthy living and loving starts with healthy thinking.

4. With intentional practice, everything can be transformed into something beautiful.

5. I'm on a quest for self-knowledge and self-understanding.

6. Serenity in, serenity out.

7. I'm learning to go green one thought at a time.

8. I can build new neural pathways that support responding rather than reacting.

9. I'm learning to let go of autopilot thinking and living.

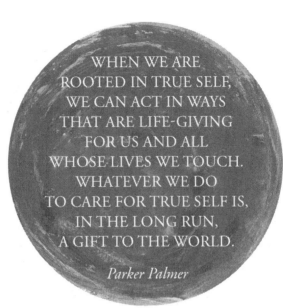

WHEN WE ARE
ROOTED IN TRUE SELF,
WE CAN ACT IN WAYS
THAT ARE LIFE-GIVING
FOR US AND ALL
WHOSE LIVES WE TOUCH.
WHATEVER WE DO
TO CARE FOR TRUE SELF IS,
IN THE LONG RUN,
A GIFT TO THE WORLD.

Parker Palmer

5

Love is a Verb:
The Selfish, Self-Care, Selfless Continuum

It was a regular day, full of errands and a long to-do list. My daughter, Jill, a junior in high school at the time, drove the car as I made calls, updated my calendar, and checked off and added items to my to-do list from the passenger seat. As we pulled into the mechanic's to get the oil changed, I made one last phone call. Jill parked and gave me a long, strange look. "Mom," she said, "who were you talking to?"

I laughed, not realizing she was even paying attention. "I was leaving myself a message on our answering machine so I wouldn't forget to finish some paperwork when we get home."

Jill was quiet for a moment. "Mom, the reason I asked who you were calling is I've *never* heard you talk like that to anyone before. You were so…mean."

All these years later I can no longer recall the exact words I left to myself on the answering machine, but I know my tone was harsh and scolding. I'd forgotten to finish that paperwork not once but twice already, and I was exasperated with myself. Caught up in the moment and already stressed, I didn't even notice my critical and dismissive tone. But my 16-year-old daughter did. Jill's comment and her incredulous stare stopped me in my tracks. Instantly I became aware of the stark difference in how I spoke to others and how I spoke to myself. I didn't realize that I treated myself so badly in my self-talk until I got caught in the act.

Dr. Kristin Neff, in her book *Self-Compassion*, offers invaluable insight on the common phenomenon of reproachful self-talk: Most of us would never speak to a friend the way we often speak to our own selves. "Self-kindness, by definition," Neff writes,

> means that we stop the constant self-judgment and disparaging internal commentary that most of us have come to see as normal. It requires us to understand our foibles and failures instead of condemning them. It entails clearly seeing the extent to which we harm ourselves through relentless self-criticism, and ending our internal war…. It involves actively comforting ourselves, responding just as we would to a dear friend in need. It means we allow ourselves to be emotionally moved by our own pain, stopping to say, 'This is really difficult right now. How can I care for and comfort myself in this moment?'[26]

Let's look at that quote in greater detail. Many of us *have* come to see our "constant self-judgment and disparaging internal commentary" as completely normal—so normal, in fact, that we *don't* see it. Even if we do, it's so habitual that we don't stop to question its validity or veracity. Yet our inner self-talk influences who we are, the choices we make, and how we interact with others. Until my teenage daughter called me out on the harsh and critical manner with which I was speaking to myself—not to mention that I was modeling for her—I had not realized the magnitude of the gap in how I treat others and how I treat myself.

Right now, take a moment to imagine some of your inner self-talk addressed aloud to a dear friend. Would it sound something like this? "Jeez, Bill, how could you be so thoughtless?" "Stacie, you idiot, I can't believe you did that *again*." One of my clients said her self-talk used to boil down to one of two words, depending on the day: stupid or ugly. When we imagine ourselves marching up to a loved one and saying those very words that we say to ourselves, it becomes immediately evident how terribly we're treating ourselves with such harsh self-talk. That kind of constant barrage of criticism undermines our self-esteem and often prevents us from being the people we want to be. "I had myself so thoroughly convinced that I was stupid," my client said, "that I just took a back seat to everything. I didn't even try, because I was already convinced I would fail, not to mention embarrass myself in the process." And inevitably, that kind of inner harm eventually emerges outward and harms others. Garbage In, Garbage Out, just as we discussed in the last chapter.

So what can we do? Let's look at the question as Neff advises—how would we respond to a dear friend in need? What would we say? My client who disparaged herself with the inner litany of "stupid" or "ugly" adopted a variation on the famous "mantra" maid Aibileen Clark teaches Skeeter in Kathryn Stockett's novel *The Help*: "You are kind. You are smart. You are beautiful."[27] That's now my client's primary belief statement.

Neff also challenges us to think of how we would care for and comfort ourselves during difficult moments. Sadly, acts of basic self-care and self-comfort are challenging for so many of us. They tend to translate to "selfish" or "self-indulgent." Yet it's just not possible to thrive without self-care. Think of it this way: If you suffered a bodily injury, would you not pause to clean and bandage the wound, or seek professional treatment if necessary? The same care is necessary for our emotional wounds. Left uncared for our wounds can't heal, and our suffering only increases.

I'd like to offer you a far more wholehearted way of looking at self-care through the lens of the **selfish —self-care —selfless continuum.** Every act towards the self falls somewhere on this continuum. As in so many things, the goal is to find the happy medium, to find the balance between two extremes on the continuum.

SELFISH   SELF-CARE   SELFLESS

As you look at this continuum, where would you place yourself?

Let's consider the two end points first. Acts that are *selfish* stop right there: with the individual self. We're selfish when we're concerned with ourselves *without regard to others.* When we are in our own, self-centered world, we develop a case of tunnel vision instead of expansiveness of vision. Wrapped up in ourselves, we end up bringing harm to others by neglecting their needs and desires.

On the other end of the continuum we find *selfless.* There is a sense in which selflessness is used positively, as synonymous with altruism. The firefighter who rushes into a burning building to rescue a person is said to have committed a "selfless act of bravery." What I'm referring to is the negative understanding of selfless—when we have *no concern or regard for ourselves.* Selfless on the selfish—self-care—selfless continuum describes a state in which we ignore the needs and desires of our own selves, or when we're excessively concerned with the needs of others at the expense of ourselves. Ignored and untended for too long, we're like a plant that's given no water or sunlight—we wither and eventually, die. Put another way, we lose ourselves, quite literally becoming self-less. The person who cares for a very ill family member around the clock may be said to be selflessly devoted to his loved one, but without time for self-care, he will become selfless in the sense of neglecting himself. Ironically, when selflessness proliferates unchecked, we burn out or become exhausted or resentful to the point that we can no longer follow through on our original desire to help others. I have many clients who come in reporting that they've lost themselves, or they don't know who they are anymore, or they can't find their "real" selves.

Operating out of either extreme—to the left of selfish or to the extreme right of selfless—seems to be acting out of a form of self-protection. Consciously or unconsciously, focusing solely on our own needs or becoming consumed with everyone else's needs can become a way to escape or ignore the journey of being real and vulnerable with ourselves, and hinder us from becoming aware of and disciplined in caring for our own needs.

The compassionate corrective to straying too far toward "selfish" or "selfless" requires reorienting ourselves to the life-giving truth that *self-care is a necessary practice for ourselves and for others*. I understand *self-care* as the measures we take and the attitudes we adopt to ensure and enhance our physical, mental, emotional, relational, spiritual and financial well-being. Self-care encompasses acts of self-compassion and self-kindness, and it requires us to let go of the self-judgment and self-criticism that inhibits our journey into wholehearted, joyful living.

Now, if all this talk of self-care and self-kindness is already making you nervous, or if your mind is already insisting that you simply don't have time for self-care, I can tell you that you're hardly alone! Sadly, there's such an overwhelming cultural bias against care of the self that even simple acts of self-care are looked upon with suspicion. Self-care is routinely confused with selfishness, self-indulgence, or even laziness. Or it's lampooned into a caricature: the pampered princess lounging about eating bonbons all day.

Yet true, life-giving self-care is anything but these oversimplified notions. Self-care is actually a *discipline* that requires time, effort, and intention. It's a learned skill that requires practice, and it calls for bravery in the face of so many voices and institutions that actively encourage us to neglect ourselves for the sake of goals such as productivity and progress.

It's time that we become aware of this kind of thinking for the harmful fallacy it is. Consider just a couple of examples. The stereotypical "Super Mom" who works full-time and volunteers for every school function and bakes all the snacks from scratch and ferries the kids to every soccer match, dental appointment, and music lesson may earn the admiration of her friends and colleagues, but she's on a fast track for exhaustion and burnout. The driven corporate striver who gets by on scant sleep (and the next day requires repeated jolts of caffeine) may earn accolades at the office, but generally, the human body isn't engineered to operate well on fewer than seven or eight hours of sleep. He or she may get a dozen more emails sent or a report finished a day earlier, but at the cost of irritability, fatigue, increased risk of illness, lack of attention to important things like family and friends, and ultimately, *lower productivity.*

Yes, our frenzy for productivity at the cost of self is actually *counterproductive.* A recent *New York Times* article titled "Relax! You'll Be More Productive" reported that "strategic renewal—including daytime workouts, short afternoon naps, longer sleep hours, more time away from the office, and longer, more frequent vacations—boosts productivity, job performance and, of course, health." The article is replete with sobering statistics and research study findings, including a Harvard study that found that sleep deprivation—defined as getting fewer than six hours of sleep per night—is costing American companies an estimated $63.2 billion annually in lost productivity.[28]

It even seems that so-called "strategic renewal" (leave it to our culture of productivity to come up with such a bureaucratic word for "rest") is hardwired into our DNA. Researchers at Florida State University studied elite performers, including musicians, athletes, actors, and chess players. They found that the best performers practiced in uninterrupted sessions of no more than 90 minutes, followed by a break. Overall these elite performers rarely work more than four and a half hours a day. "'To maximize gains from long-term practice,' the lead researcher concluded, 'individuals must avoid exhaustion and must limit practice to an amount from which they can *completely recover on a daily or weekly basis* [emphasis mine]'."[29] Now *that* is an act of self-care—and it also happens to produce performance results that are far higher than if we had not paused to practice self-care.

It's time that we give ourselves permission to engage in regular self-care. The old analogy we hear about putting on our own oxygen masks before assisting others is so accurate. Once space opens up in our hearts due to self-compassion and self-care, then we'll have more available for others. You really *can't* give away what you don't have, and if we're not regularly practicing self-care we can't be effective in our jobs and can't be fully present in our personal lives.

And we simply won't be as happy and content. Many advocates of self-care encourage caring for the self in order to care for others. And while this *is* one of the huge benefits of self-care, I want to make sure you know that self-care is a worthy practice in and of itself, just for you. Whoever you are, whatever you do or haven't done, you deserve to feel healthy, mentally clear, joyful, loved, and deeply connected just because you're you. "I thought I had to *earn* any down time for myself," said Marika, a 36-year-old accounting executive. "Like *first* I'd get a promotion and *then* I'd reward myself with a vacation, or *first* I'd finish a huge project and *then* I'd go for a run. But I had it exactly backwards. By the time I finished the project I was too exhausted to run, and by the time I earned my promotion I felt too busy to stop. It was that way with everything, until I just burnt out from overwork and ultimately ended up leaving what I thought was my 'dream job' by the time I was 30. Now I know to do small but impactful acts of self-care all along so I can be the person I want to be and be energized and effective at my job."

In my profession, which entails listening to people's difficult life stories and to hearts that are aching, I consider it part of my job description to engage in regular self-care. I have learned that self-care is a non-negotiable for me. Counseling is a joy and a privilege, but it gives me a front-row seat to all manner of suffering, which can take a psychological toll unless I'm intentionally giving myself a break in order to recharge and be fully present to each client. Simply put, if I'm not practicing self-care, I'm not an effective therapist. In addition, it's a "practice what I preach" value, because I regularly teach clients the self-care continuum.

Here are my go-to forms of self-care: 1) My husband Roger and I have conversations over dinner about how our days went. 2) I talk with family and friends often. 3) I practice Stop Breathe Believe. 4) I practice centering prayer on a regular basis. 5) I receive spiritual direction once a month. 6) I get up early to give myself the gift of two hours of solitude, during which I read, pray, exercise, and/or journal. 7) I laugh and dance. 8) I get a massage once a month.

During our **dinner conversations**, Roger and I don't give each other meticulous reports of our days. But we do share a general overview and any special joys or concerns that arose; this allows both of us to unwind and offload the stresses of the day, and simply enjoy time together. It's a form of individual self-care as well as self-care as a couple. Early in our marriage when we had young children, Roger was required to go on annual weekend conferences with his company, and I always accompanied him. Yes, I sometimes felt guilty about leaving the kids behind. But it allowed Justin and Jill to spend time with their grandparents who adored them, and it allowed Roger and me a few days on our own. On those weekend excursions we'd fall in love all over again, so early in our relationship we learned the value of intentionally setting time apart for ourselves. We attribute a big part of the depth of our marriage to those weekends away and the lessons we learned about self-care as a couple. Any guilt I felt at first about leaving the children behind melted away as I inevitably returned more relaxed, more rejuvenated, and eager to be reunited with the kids.

For me, **keeping in regular touch with my family and friends** is also an important form of self-care. As an extrovert I love interacting with people, and I love staying in touch and maintaining connections. The deep connection with family and friends is life-giving.

Stop Breathe Believe is my primary awareness practice. If I'm feeling drained or that something is amiss, I stop my activity, reorient myself with calming breathwork, and set a new intention for whatever form of self-care seems to be called for. Recently, for instance, I found myself overwhelmed and stressed at the prospect of a week full of regular clients, writing this book, and a weekend workshop. So as the tension mounted I set aside the stack of paperwork I was about to tackle, said, "Stop, Dianne," and took ten deep, slow breaths. I then encouraged myself to take it one day at a time, and I practiced another quick act of self-care by jotting down three things I was grateful for about that week. Within two minutes I had a list of items that reminded me of what a privilege it is to do what I love and love what I do. I feel honored and humbled to walk alongside others and listen to their difficult stories. I also set an intention to be more intentional about the number of things that show up on my weekly calendar!

Regular prayer and **monthly spiritual direction** are the times when, instead of pouring myself out for others, I let someone pour into me. During centering prayer that Someone is God; during spiritual direction it's a wise and trusted mentor. I don't have to do anything during these sacred times other than show up and be open and receptive. I can count on these times to be life-giving and restorative. In addition, spiritual direction is a place of accountability for me regarding my schedule. I struggle with getting over-committed and I need stabilizing, grounding forces in place to help me maintain focus and a reasonable balance.

The **two hours I set aside most mornings** for various self-care activities have become such a cherished time. Two hours may sound like a lot, but it's time that I fight for in my schedule, and it readies me to be fully present to the people I encounter, in a professional or personal capacity. It's how I center myself, and it's the platform from which I go forth. I'm also at a stage in life—with adult children out of the house and a flexible work schedule—that I'm able to manage my time in this way. There's a sacred rhythm for each of us, and a time and place for everything. I encourage you to pay attention to what's realistic and doable for you. I devote my morning "alone time" to prayer, exercise, reading, and/or journaling. To me journaling is one of the healthiest things we can do—just let life flow through the pen unfiltered. I find that the simple act of getting my thoughts and feelings onto paper is in itself therapeutic, and often, I make connections and gain insights that I wouldn't have otherwise. Writing longhand forces me to slow down, and it's a fantastic form of self-care.

As for **laughing** and **dancing**, I simply try to do both every chance I get! Laughter is born from the same deep place as weeping, and the emotional release it provides is invigorating and just plain fun. Roger and I love to dance, and I also dance alone at home. I have a favorite spot where the sun shines in the entry hall, and dancing with joy is a very spiritual activity for me.

Finally, I get a **massage** once a month. I have cherished memories from girlhood of lying on my grandmother's green couch while she gave me a backrub. There's something so healing about touch. It's well known that babies deprived of human touch will develop slowly or even die; human contact is so important to physical and emotional wellness that Neonatal Intensive Care Units now regularly engage volunteers to hold, cuddle, rock and talk to the infants in their care. Then there are many healing modalities that are based on the proven wisdom that touch is restorative. Healing touch and therapeutic massage can reduce stress, ease pain, lower blood pressure, boost immune function and promote faster healing.[30] I have one client, a widow, who says sometimes she goes to church just so she can receive hugs.

Now, about that monthly massage, I have a confession. Despite knowing all the benefits of human touch, it took me a while to become comfortable with this particular form of self-care. The first few times I went, I parked my car far enough away from the office that if someone I knew happened to pass by, they wouldn't know I was "indulging" in a massage. My uneasiness didn't even stop there. I waited in my car until there was no one in sight so no one would see me enter the massage therapist's office. I couldn't even let strangers I'd never see again possibly think I was self-indulgent! *That's* the power of our cultural bias against self-care. It can be hard work indeed to act against systemic opposition to self-care.

As we're so accustomed to confusing self-care with selfishness, it's important to remember that *any act of self-care or self-compassion will at first feel like an act of selfishness*. My first couple of massages certainly felt selfish—until I realized how the stress relief and rejuvenation I received always positively affected my interactions with others. The new mom who hires a sitter so she can go run errands or meet up with her friends may feel selfish. Yet that choice to care for herself is critical to her ability to effectively handle the rigors of caring for a newborn, and the emotional boost she'll receive from social interaction and a respite from caretaking will allow her to be more fully present to her baby upon her return. The person who breaks off a codependent or abusive relationship may feel selfish, but getting out is necessary for his or her well-being and personal development, and a life-giving act of bravery. Saying no can often feel selfish. But habitually overextending ourselves stretches us to a breaking point and eventually leads to burnout, resentment, and even illness. It's also a near-guarantee that we'll perform many tasks with mediocrity rather than a few well-chosen tasks with excellence.

That's the major difference between selfishness and self-care: the benefits of self-care *always* extend beyond the self. If we're caring for ourselves, we're able to care for others. Simple as that. As we get better at self-care—and remember, it's something that must be practiced, like any new skill—our acts of self-care will come to feel like acts of selflessness in the positive sense. And self-care results in a beautiful ripple effect that can unleash compassion into the world farther than we ever dreamed possible.

There's no doubt about it: We're our best selves if we're giving our best effort to self-care, and we live life best if we're practicing regular self-care. Everyone benefits.

BEFRIENDING YOUR BODY

There are endless ways we neglect to extend the care and compassion our bodies need. We routinely deprive ourselves of sleep in order to get more done. We convince ourselves we don't have time to exercise and spend more time at our desks or in our recliners. On the other extreme, we can allow an exercise routine to get out of hand by pushing past a healthy endurance level and getting injured. We neglect to make and follow through with medical checkups because we can't cram another thing into an already overburdened schedule. We're so busy we often skip breakfast, or get through the day on energy drinks and a power bar. We're so stressed we seek quick-fix comforts like smoking, alcohol, drugs, or overeating.

We can keep up unhealthy routines like these for a while, but the body can only be ignored for so long. It *will* make its complaints known! At first its murmurings are subtle: a crick in the neck, a mild headache, sniffles, an upset stomach, aching feet. Ignored, our body's cues do what anyone would do to be heard—they grow louder. The crick in the neck becomes chronic and even debilitating. The upset stomach escalates into irritable bowel syndrome. The headache becomes a migraine. The sniffles become a full-blown cold that knocks us out for a week.

Your body is a habitual truth-teller. It's incapable of lying, and it's *always* speaking. Many holistic practices and therapeutic models recognize that our minds and our bodies are intimately related, and that every part of us works together in an intricate, seamless dance. Our particular challenge in our noisy, fast-paced 21st century is that so many of us don't learn to tune in and listen to our bodies, or we ignore its signals because we "just don't have the time" to listen. You may have heard before that the words LISTEN and SILENT contain the exact same letters. There's a wonderful clue there: When we become silent, we can truly listen. You cannot listen to your inner self or to your body while always on the run.

For many of us, it's become necessary to form a specific intention to check in with our bodies. During the "breathe" portion of Stop Breathe Believe, practice a body scan. If you're able, lie down on your back; if not, sitting with back straight and feet flat on the floor will be just fine. Now, starting with your toes and moving up toward the crown of your head, mentally check in with each part of your body. Go slowly, allowing each part of the body to speak to you. What does it have to say? Is there any area that aches? Tingles? Yearns to be touched? Feels numb? Seems perfectly content? Feels tight or tense? We all carry our stress in different parts of our bodies. Mine is in my neck and shoulders. If I let my stress level go too far, at some point the tension demands to be heard: The muscles of my shoulders are knotted and tight, and my neck aches. At that point I do a relaxation exercise. Sometimes it's Stop Breathe Believe so I can identify and redirect the negative thought that's got me stressed out. Sometimes I'll give myself a short shoulder or temple massage; head and neck rolls can also help release tension. If I have the time and opportunity, I go for a walk or do yoga. I pray or meditate. I journal. I call up a friend and talk.

Another thing to try is a visual exercise I've used with my clients for years and now use with participants in The Daring Way™ workshops that Nancy Schornack, a colleague, and I teach together. Using markers and a simple drawing of the human body, we ask participants to draw, in whatever way they like, what they're feeling in their bodies. (I use the classic gingerbread man outline for this exercise; you can find one in Appendix III on page 182). Or sometimes, I use the drawing to address a specific issue; I'll ask clients where in their body they feel shame or anxiety, for instance. One client's gingerbread man stands out in my mind. Naya handed over her gingerbread man worksheet and she shared visually what she had not "seen" before—at least 80% of the body was tattooed with colorful markings. The top of the head was covered with angry red and black slashes. The eyes were blocked out by blue X's, and over the mouth she'd drawn a black zipper. The neck and shoulders were stippled with red dots. Over both lungs was the ubiquitous *NO* symbol—the red circle with a red slash through it. The stomach was colored in with green loops and squiggles. Over the genital area was a giant black X. And the feet were covered entirely with two heavy-looking rectangles that Naya had colored in gray.

I asked her to tell me about each part of her drawing, and she led me through a bodily tour of her shame. The black slashes on her head were the shaming thoughts that filled her mind on a daily basis; the red slashes represented a tension headache. The blue X's over her eyes represented her inability to cry. The red dots on her neck and shoulders recorded areas of tension. The *NO* symbol over her lungs indicated that her chest felt tight and that she was breathing shallow breaths. The green loops and squiggles of her stomach indicated queasiness and nausea. The giant black X over the genital area indicated her repressed sexuality, and that in her deeply conservative family she'd been made to feel so much shame over her sexual impulses. Finally, the gray rectangles over her feet were two concrete blocks that represented her experience of feeling stuck and weighed down.

And do you know what's perhaps even more fascinating about Naya's somatic exercise? She had come to therapy for help in overcoming social and performance anxiety. In other words, the issue she initially identified as the primary impediment to her version of wholehearted living was anxiety. As we got deeper into her story and listened to her *body*, she was able to identify some long-seated issues with shame and get to the root of her anxiety. Naya had grown up in a deeply shame-based culture, and she felt inferior and unworthy. The somatic exercise revealed the root causes of her anxiety and thus sparked the beginning of growth and healing that unfolded on a holistic level.

PRACTICING NON-JUDGMENT

Another huge part of self-care and self-compassion is the practice of non-judgment. Non-judgment is yet another skill that we must practice and which we can progressively improve. My awakening to the need for non-judgment, in myself and in others, arrived when and where so many wonderful life lessons have: during a session in my office.

Ellen's tendency to judge others had created lots of problems in her life. Her performance evaluations often cited her challenges in getting along with colleagues and her inability to be a team player. At home, she and her husband often argued over her "constant harping," in his words. ("She's *constantly* on my case," Jeff said at their first appointment. "I can't do anything right.") Fortunately Ellen was well aware of her judgmental nature and really wanted to move toward a more compassionate way of being in the world and interacting with others. She practiced Stop Breathe Believe in order to stop herself the second she became aware of a critical thought, regain her focus, and redirect that judgment to something generous and compassionate. At about that same time I began working with Ellen and Jeff, I happened to be reading several books that underscored how common it is to judge others, and how judgment creeps up in ways we'd never notice. Here's an incisive passage on judging others from Brené Brown's *I Thought it Was Just Me (But It Isn't)* that really hit home:

> Most of us are one paycheck, one divorce, one drug-addicted kid, one mental health diagnosis, one serious illness, one sexual assault, one drinking binge, one night of unprotected sex, or one affair away from being 'those people'—the ones we don't trust, the ones we pity, the ones we don't let our children play with, the ones bad things happen to, the ones we don't want living next door.[31]

After weeks of using Stop Breathe Believe, Ellen was finding the practice very effective in helping her redirect her critical judgments to a more open-minded, compassionate view. Further, because she wasn't *voicing* as many of her criticisms, she and her husband were getting along much better. Something clicked for me and I realized, *Wow! Stop Breathe Believe might help me with this too!* That very day I set an intention that for one year, I would practice suspending judgment towards others. It was a fascinating year. With the practice of Stop, I began to catch myself being judgmental of someone's hairstyle, someone's faith practice, someone's decision, someone's choice of mate, someone's reaction in a group discussion. I'm sad to say that the list went on. But as I became aware of a particular judgment towards another, I was then able to take a deep breath and be intentional with letting that judgment go. Finally, as I released that judgment, I came up with a green statement that replaced the judgment with a more expansive perspective of acceptance and empathy.

By the end of that year, my compassion toward others had increased by magnitudes, and I had let go of lots of emotional garbage—all the gunk that was clogging my "love others as you would yourself" arteries. But what also became deeply apparent to me was how often I harshly judged and criticized myself. Clearly I was in need of another year-long project!

So I set another intention, and as it turns out, the year of suspending judgment toward myself was *far* more difficult than a year of suspending judgment toward others. The clothesline of thoughts running through my head looked something like this: "I can't believe you thought that!" "Dianne, how do you know anything about her underlying motives?" "How in the world could you have said such a thing?" "There you go again, jumping to conclusions."

But precisely because I'd *practiced* letting go of judgments and replacing them with a compassionate thought, I began practicing the same grace toward myself. When I caught myself in a harsh self-judgment, I responded with *It's okay, Dianne* or *You are so human* or *I'm learning to increase my self-compassion.* Through my intentional and focused practice of self-compassion, I was able to discover a new depth of love for myself. Not in a narcissistic, "I've got it all together" way, but in a way that gave me greater self-forgiveness and greater motivation to try and try again. When I fail in the area of judgment—and I continue to fail and try again—I simply acknowledge the slip-up, take several deep breaths to bring myself back to the place of love and compassion from which I want to operate and where I want to dwell, and then go forward with a belief statement. The –ing belief statements help tremendously. "I'm *learning* to be more compassionate toward myself." "I'm *practicing* a new way of being kind." "I'm *enacting* the truth that love is a verb." Sometimes I place my hand over my heart in a physical act of self-kindness, just as I would pat someone on the shoulder or give a hug. The power of touch is so huge, and even this small act of self-kindness can be a belief statement in action.

Ultimately, my ability to look upon myself less judgmentally and with greater compassion enables me to look upon others with less judgment and with greater compassion. And it goes both ways; my ability to be less judgmental of others and have more compassion for others enabled me to become less judgmental of myself and find greater self-compassion within my own heart. This beautiful give-and-receive between self and others is mutually informing; each enhances and sustains the other.

SUGGESTIONS FOR PRACTICING SELF-CARE

The discipline of self-care puts words and action to the concept of *Love is a Verb.* If you're not accustomed to practicing self-care, it may take a few attempts to find just the forms of self-care that leave you refreshed, rejuvenated, and restored. Don't be discouraged—in fact, have fun with trying out new things! Start small. Remember that as you first move toward the self-care marker on the continuum, acts of self-care may *feel* selfish. But stick with it: Self-care is a non-negotiable for you and the people in your life.

Do what you can with what you have. Appendix II (page 185) offers suggestions for practicing self-care. If planning a party feels overwhelming but you need some friend time, go to coffee with a friend. If pumping iron at the gym seems out of reach, go for a walk around the neighborhood. If spending twenty minutes in meditation looks unlikely, turn the radio on to an instrumental station while you run your errands. If the schedule seems too tight for a nice dinner, call the pizza hotline (we had the pizza number memorized during those fun, crazy, zany years of sports/theatre/ school activities when Justin and Jill were in middle school and high school). Start with small steps and recognize that honoring the value of self-care as a part of your lifestyle is important. Savor the moment of *wherever* you are and *whatever* you are doing—that too can be self-care.

SOME BELIEF STATEMENTS TO SUPPORT YOUR SELF-CARE PRACTICE

1. Letting go of self-judgment is an invaluable act of self-kindness.

2. I'm beginning to believe that I am worthy of caring for myself as I would others.

3. Self-care is a necessary practice for myself and others.

4. Acts of self-care can help me move past stuck places.

5. I'm learning to learn from my body.

6. Self-care is my birthright, not something that must be earned.

7. It will be fun to learn new ways to care for myself.

8. Sometimes self-care means letting others take the reins.

9. I'm learning to voice my needs.

WE DO NOT
HAVE TO IMPROVE
OURSELVES;
WE JUST
HAVE TO LET GO OF
WHAT BLOCKS
OUR HEART.

Jack Kornfield

6

The Overwhelmed Pie

Early one May, as the blustery Iowa winds had finally given way to spring warmth, I arrived at a local university to offer a workshop for a sorority. Students hurried to classes, and one group, well dressed and carrying portfolios and briefcases, streamed into the student center. A sign by the door revealed what was going on inside: a job fair. The next generation of graduates was about to hit the job market, just as headlines were announcing a downward trend in hiring. Students were days away from finals and commencement celebrations. There was a buzz everywhere, it seemed, everyone rushing to complete their own personal to-do lists.

I had my own kind of frantic dance going on. In two days I was traveling to Texas to see my extended family, and as anyone who's packed for a two-week trip knows, there are a thousand and one things to be done. And professionally, my schedule was full to overflowing.

Which is what had brought me to the university. The topic of the workshop for the day? Stress management. Oh yes, there really are no coincidences—*hello*, Dianne!

I was glad I arrived a bit early because I needed a little stress management myself. I turned off the car and closed my eyes. "Okay, *stop*, Dianne," I said aloud to myself. "Stop." The word was both a benevolent command and permission to let go. I *could* stop the swirl of thoughts that were keeping me from being present to *this* moment, at *this* time and place. Briefly, I glanced at the thoughts I'd caught. *How will I get it all done? Which to-do item should I tackle next? I'm apprehensive about this workshop.*

Bingo. That was the single thought I needed to address in this moment. My apprehension about the workshop had nothing at all to do with my abilities or what I had to say or a lack of preparation. It was all about being so stressed out and preoccupied that I couldn't focus on any of the individual tasks facing me with the presence and intention I wanted to have.

Recalling a yoga technique, I decided to "breathe into" that apprehension. If you're holding a pose and find a part of your body tense or stretched to the limit, you *breathe into* the tight spot, giving the area that needs attention the gift of intentional, relaxing breath and invigorating oxygen. Of course you never push to the point of pain, but the technique is surprisingly effective in loosening up stiff muscles and helping to hold a challenging pose. So, holding the *one thought* of my apprehension in mind, I took several deep breaths, directing each inhalation to that initial stage of nervousness, and with each exhalation, letting go of a little more of it. My belief statement was simple yet powerful: "I can be fully present." That statement encompassed everything: If I could be *fully* present to the job of giving this workshop, and *fully* present as the young women shared and asked questions, I would be effective and truly helpful.

The entire sequence of this "micro-meditation" form of Stop Breathe Believe took me less time to do than it took you to read about it. But it was all I needed. I had stopped my unhealthy thinking in its tracks, given myself a good dose of serenity, and reoriented myself to one of my overall life goals of being fully present to each moment. I'd take all of this with me as I addressed the sorority.

Forty-five beautiful young women from the ages of 18 to 22 waited in the common room of the sorority house. I did a short introductory presentation on Stop Breathe Believe and then asked the girls to share some of their sources of stress. They didn't hesitate! Here's a *partial* list of stressors they called out within minutes:

- **School**—upcoming finals, grades they weren't pleased with or were worried about
- **The Future**—deciding on a major, graduate school, internships, finding a job, finding an apartment and/or roommate after graduation
- **Relationships with Significant Others**—breakups, long-distance relationships, worry over not being in a relationship, rejection, roommate issues, sex

- **Physical Appearance**—the ever-present pressure to be attractive, specific physical concerns or complaints
- **Family Issues**—tense or broken relationships with family members
- **Financial Issues**—impending school loan repayments, financial burdens on family

As the list of stressors continued to pour in, one young woman jokingly called out, "Save us, Ms. Jones! We need help!" The room broke into laughter, and it had such a relaxing effect on everyone that I decided to add more laughter to the presentation. I had everyone stand up, and then led the group in a quick laughter yoga exercise designed to elicit deep, healing belly laughter. For this group I chose the handshake exercise. Everyone moved around the room shaking hands with one another, pretending to spread a healthful "laughter infection" as they made contact. If you don't mind looking a little silly for a few minutes, the laughter that is at first contrived soon becomes genuine and spontaneous. And as laughter is contagious in the best possible way, giggles and laughter quickly swept through the room. When we returned to our seats, the energy in the room was palpably different—we were all refreshed and relaxed.[32]

It struck me that it was time to deviate from the speech I'd prepared. "All right, y'all," I said, "it's time for Overwhelmed Pie."

I don't know if it was the crazy name or my deep Texas accent, but the room burst into laughter again. I was thrilled. Laughter is one of the very best ways to treat ourselves to some quick, effective stress relief, and it showed me that the group was relaxed and thus more internally prepared to do some vulnerable emotional work.

The Overwhelmed Pie is a tool I use with clients—and myself—when life gets uncomfortably complicated and stressful. It's an easy, effective way to identify and *differentiate* your sources of stress so you can address them *one by one*, just like Stop Breathe Believe helps you to identify and address one thought at a time. Few people can sit down and eat an entire pie—and if they did, they'd feel sick afterward. But we *can* enjoy a pie slice by slice over a reasonable period of time, and it's far more enjoyable that way. Would you rather savor one delicious slice, or end up sick from scarfing down an entire pie?

Or think of it this way: Who wants to eat a blueberry-apple-rhubarb-raisin-chocolate-lemon meringue-pecan pie? When it feels like *everything* is coming at us at once, our "pie" suddenly looks and tastes like a nauseating mix. Some people call this experience a perfect storm or a quagmire or an impasse (or other terms that are unprintable). I call it the Overwhelmed Pie.

The good news about the Overwhelmed Pie is that it not only pinpoints the source of the issues that are hindering you, but coupled with Stop Breathe Believe it shows you a way to overcome them. Here's how it works.

Draw a pie chart with six or eight slices of pie. Now assign your sources of stress to each slice. At the workshop I passed out blank sheets of paper and markers and the sorority sisters enthusiastically dove in. I asked for a volunteer to share hers. A senior I'll call Ashley offered her diagram:

ASHLEY'S OVERWHELMED PIE

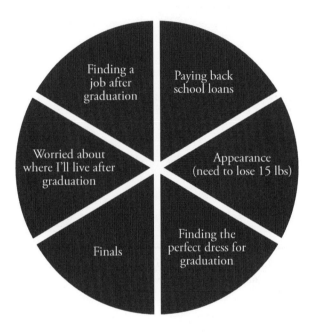

"Wow," I said, "that's a lot, isn't it, Ashley?" I thanked Ashley for her courage to share and congratulated her on her keen self-awareness. She knew exactly what was causing her stress, and she was able to name it. Still, most of these were very broad categories she'd identified, and the next step with Overwhelmed Pie is to break down each stressor into manageable components that can be addressed. "Finding a job," for example, is an entire Overwhelmed Pie in itself—you can't "eat" that issue in one sitting. You can, however, break that down into slices that can be managed over a reasonable span of time: polish résumé, network, research job openings, set up interviews, and so on.

"Okay," I said, "to show y'all what to do with this, let's use the appearance slice. Anyone else have an 'appearance' slice on their Overwhelmed Pie?" A chorus of yeses filled the room and nearly every hand went up.

I explained that appearance was such a complex and enduring issue (not to mention so unique to each person) that it constituted its *own* Overwhelmed Pie, and we needed to separate out all the factors feeding into worry and stress over physical appearance. "So step two is to pie it out," I said.

Credit for using "pie" as a verb goes to a client of mine who relies on Overwhelmed Pie to work her way through every perfect storm that comes her way. It made immediate sense to me, and now I routinely "pie it out."

To "pie out" one slice of your original Overwhelmed Pie, simply draw a line from that section of your pie to a new pie, and then break down that original slice into its components. As a group, we came up with *two* new pies for the "appearance" slice, one concentrating on external actions that could contribute to health and wellness, and the other representing the much deeper, interior work that needed to occur in order to feel beautiful no matter what. The external pie looked like this, and was largely the same for many of the girls:

APPEARANCE—EXTERNALS

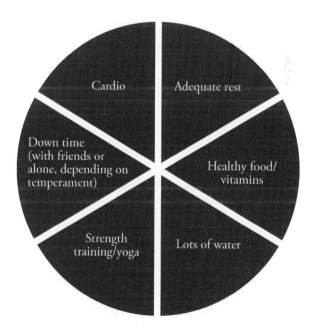

This pie identified a list of concrete steps to take. The advantage here is that actionable tasks do lead you toward your goal, and having a plan written down gives you a sense of control when things are spinning out of control. It also gives you accountability in seeing those goals through. The disadvantage would occur if this pie became just another to-do list. I wanted the girls to move beyond externals and get closer to the roots of why so many of them—all attractive, smart young women with loads of potential—struggled with feeling unattractive. And that's exactly where the second Overwhelmed Pie came in.

"What would lead you to think that you're not beautiful already?" I asked.

The boisterous room fell silent. "Let me put it another way," I said. "Let's just quiet ourselves for a moment, and let's practice Stop Breathe Believe and become aware of what it is we're thinking about our appearance. So close your eyes, and let's come to that place of inner awareness about appearance. Maybe you need to picture yourself standing in front of the mirror. Listen to your own self-talk—what is it you're saying to yourself as you look in the mirror? What's the story you're telling yourself about how you're *supposed* to look?"

After a few moments of silence, one woman spoke up. "My story says I'll get rejected if I'm not thin. By, like, *everyone*."

More answers tumbled out.

"Mine says I have to look like my sister—she's taller and naturally blond, and my parents always liked her best."

"Well my parents have been telling me I needed a nose job since I was fourteen!" another woman said. "Try getting *that* out of your head."

"I'm always telling myself that my skin is too dark."

"I'm ashamed of the cellulite on my thighs."

"Cultural messages are all over my self-talk," one woman said. "Like I'm somehow less than if I don't look like some Photoshopped model."

A vigorous and liberating discussion ensued as the group shared their self-talk around appearance and "vented" about the ways it had hindered them from a sense of wholeness and happiness. Eventually Ashley re-entered the discussion. "Well hey," she said, "can we get some of *this* stuff on paper—can we pie this out?"

And that's just what we did. Each young woman who chose to do so drew a second Overwhelmed Pie for her "appearance" slice, this one focused on the internal self-talk that powered her apprehensions about physical appearance. Those who didn't cite appearance as a primary concern chose another issue. One young woman, for example, "pied out" her stress over finals, using one pie to assign exam dates and subjects to each slice, and another to identify individual goals that had to be met in order to study sufficiently for each.

Several of the sorority sisters shared their Overwhelmed Pie diagrams relating to self-talk and appearance, and I found myself incredibly moved by their honesty and vulnerability. Space doesn't permit me to reproduce all of their diagrams, so again I'll share Ashley's.

APPEARANCE—INTERNAL AWARENESS

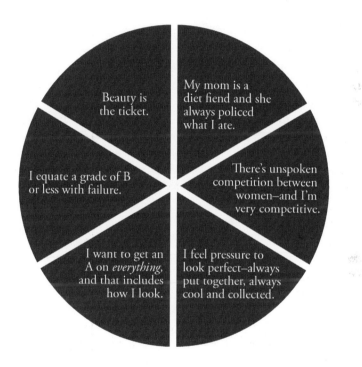

By the time we got to slice #6 Ashley was in tears, and so were many of her sorority sisters. It was clear that this was a close, supportive group of women, and that many of them could identify with what she was saying. "I never put that issue with the grades and appearance together before," Ashley said. "I've always been driven and I've always made good grades, but I didn't realize I was taking a mentality of *I've got to get straight A's* into *all* of my life and trying to prove I wasn't a failure. I think I was so busy exercising and dieting that I didn't slow down long enough to listen to any of my self-talk and even wonder if it was *true*."

Ashley had honed in exactly on the most useful aspect of Overwhelmed Pie. You may have to "pie it out" into six or eight pies from your original one, but if you follow those sources of stress through to the seeds of their origination, Overwhelmed Pie can reveal unconscious apprehensions and blocks. It was amazing to actually watch this happen right in front of us that day at the workshop. Ashley inspired me, and she inspired her entire sorority as well.

Before I left, I wanted to leave the group with some direction for going forward. We now needed belief statements to speak to and heal the sources of stress and negative self-talk we'd identified. Several participants generously shared their negative self-talk and their belief statements. To come full circle with Stop Breathe Believe, we wrote them in the language of red thoughts/green thoughts.

> **Red Thought**: I couldn't get my jeans buttoned so I'm a failure.
> **Green Thought**: No jean size determines my worth.

> **Red Thought**: I don't look like the typical all-American beauty.
> **Green Thought**: I am learning to see my unique self as beautiful.

> **Red Thought**: My mother routinely points out my physical flaws.
> **Green Thought**: I am choosing not to accept others' insecurities as my own.

> **Red Thought**: I'm flat-chested.
> **Green Thought**: The size of my breasts is not the barometer of beauty.

> **Red Thought**: My complexion sucks.
> **Green Thought**: I want to learn how to be friends with my skin.

> **Red Thought**: I am not thin enough.
> **Green Thought**: I want to be the real, healthy me.

> **Red Thought**: I can list 25 physical flaws off the top of my head.
> **Green Thought**: Stop.

If you haven't already, notice a very interesting thing about these red thought/green thought pairings: In nearly every case, the red thought was based upon an external worry. *But the green thought that leads to healing comes from within.* It takes a change in thinking, a shift in perspective, to return to the path of wholeness, and this can happen one thought at a time.

Further, as is so often the case, the external event that's causing us such stress is not the true issue. The young woman whose parents wanted her to get a nose job expressed this beautifully. "It's not like my relationship with my parents is going to be suddenly perfect if I have plastic surgery," she said. "Really, my nose isn't the issue *at all*. My parents have their own hang-ups, and I'm not going to take them on. Who cares about the bump on my nose—that *hello*, I actually *like* because it makes me different."

The entire room broke into spontaneous applause after she spoke. I could not have been more proud of these young women, and I was so moved by their courage and honesty I found myself on the verge of tears.

I thanked the sorority sisters for their time and attention, and invited them to begin practicing Stop Breathe Believe as they encountered stoplights, and to take with them everything they'd learned from Overwhelmed Pie and to practice it when life became intense. I told them that I'd had clients who used the combination of Stop Breathe Believe and Overwhelmed Pie to get through everything from grad school exams, to divorce, to starting a new job, to dealing with a lawsuit, to the struggle of living with an alcoholic partner, to being a single mom with umpteen pieces of life to deal with—anything that's overwhelming.

When our son Justin was in law school, for example, he used the Overwhelmed Pie as a tool to manage his amount of coursework and the staggering preparation for year-end finals. Because there aren't multiple tests per course, but *one* test for each course, *one* chance to score well, the degree of stress is extremely high. So imagine his dismay when he sat down to one particular exam and discovered that the format was completely different from what he'd expected. After a moment of panic, he took the first few minutes of a 3-hour "every second counts exam" and drew a pie chart on the top right of his paper to quickly recalibrate his plan. Later that day, he called and said, "Mom, the Overwhelmed Pie works! I might have been stressed out about my misunderstanding of the structure of the test, but I had a tool that worked to break it down to manageable tasks." I can't take credit for his success in law school, but I will take credit for one crazy way to serve pie to your son!

"My clients' challenges aren't easy," I said to the coeds, "and Stop Breathe Believe isn't a magical potion, but they're making it and doing great. One day at a time, one thought at a time."

"Maybe that's because they're pieing it out!" Ashley said with a big grin.

The room broke into applause for her, and no one clapped harder than I did.

GREEN THOUGHTS FOR ENJOYING YOUR PIE

1. There's no one, single way to slice a pie.
2. I'm choosing not to internalize others' problems.
3. Healing and wholeness can come from within.
4. I'm learning to live in the here and now.
5. I'm learning to discern the truth in my own self-talk.
6. When I separate the pie into pieces, I feel calmer.
7. I can savor the taste of each moment when I take one bite at a time.
8. One day at a time, one thought at a time.
9. I'm learning to be fully present to each moment.

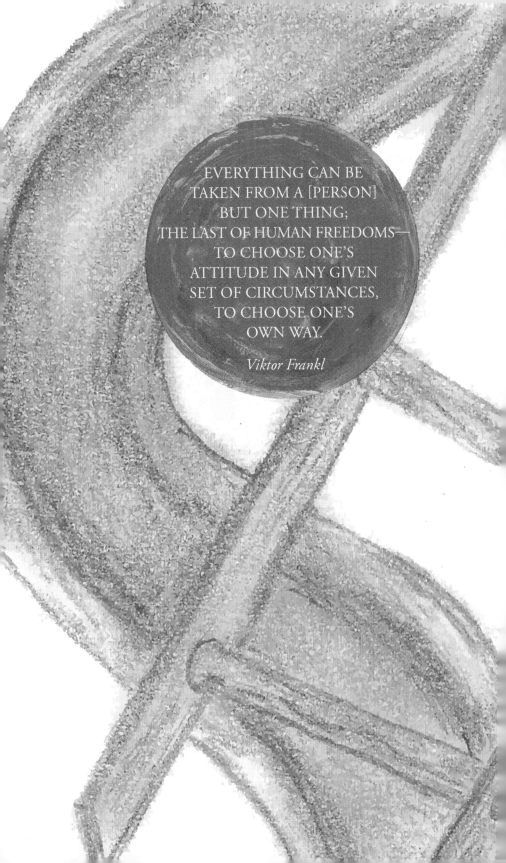

EVERYTHING CAN BE
TAKEN FROM A [PERSON]
BUT ONE THING;
THE LAST OF HUMAN FREEDOMS—
TO CHOOSE ONE'S
ATTITUDE IN ANY GIVEN
SET OF CIRCUMSTANCES,
TO CHOOSE ONE'S
OWN WAY.

Viktor Frankl

7
Chutes and Ladders

Suzy's husband was convicted of fraud and racketeering and she wakes every morning to find her family's story in the headlines. Some of her closest friends have shunned her, and she dreads going out in public.

Angela was in therapy for six months before she admitted she'd been having an affair for the past three years.

Carl painfully confided that he and his wife hadn't had sex in more than four years.

"I mispronounced the name of our new client at the board meeting and my assistant corrected me in front of everyone," said Veronica. "I can't stop replaying the scene in my head. I even find myself saying 'Idiot!' out loud from time to time."

Bill revealed that he'd been fired and hadn't yet told his family or friends. Every morning he left the house at the usual time and returned in the evenings. He had no idea how long he planned to keep up the ruse.

After attending her first women's book club meeting, Deborah came in to her therapy appointment crying. "They were all in designer clothes and everyone's hair and nails were *perfect*," she said. "I don't fit in there at all."

Or here's a story about me—I join the gym or yoga studio with good intentions of going regularly and then get busy with other things and don't go. I reprimand myself for wasting money and not following through on my goals. I conclude that I'm undisciplined and can't follow through with anything.

Do you see the common theme in these anecdotes? If not, here are a few more that continue to tell the story.

"I always feel like the outsider looking in."

"I'm drowning as a Mom—the loneliness, the schedules, the lack of affirmation."

"I'm addicted to prescription painkillers."

"I'm the only one in my circle of friends who doesn't have a college degree."

"I am not respected at the office, even though I'm the boss."

"My own family doesn't accept me or even let me hug them because I am gay."

"I have no idea how to keep up with all I need to know about technology."

"I really don't want children."

As widely divergent as these stories are, they share a key emotion found within every culture and every population. It's an emotion that's so painful and potentially so destructive that no one wants to experience it and few want to talk about it. *Shame.*[33]

As painful as shame is it's natural to want to avoid it or try and ignore it in the hopes it will just go away. But if there's anything we need to recognize and respond to mindfully, it's the insidious force of shame. Whether we're aware of it or not, shame is a prevalent force in all of our lives, and it lies at the root of so many of our challenges and growing edges. I'm absolutely passionate about helping people understand shame because it's key to moving through so many of the roadblocks preventing us from living wholehearted, integrated and authentic lives. Recognizing and moving through shame *constructively* rather than getting "shame-struck and stuck" can revolutionize our self-perception, our relationships with other people, and the choices we make.

Though we all have some sense of what shame is, it can be challenging to recognize it in our lives and difficult to define because we're so motivated to avoid it. As we enter into a discussion about recognizing shame and how to respond, it is important to define our terms.

Dr. Brené Brown, author of *Daring Greatly* and shame researcher at the University of Houston, has done pioneering work in the area of shame. According to Brown, shame is "the intensely painful feeling or experience of believing that we are flawed and therefore unworthy of love and belonging."[34] It's a profoundly isolating experience. Take another look at the last part of Brown's definition: When we feel shame, we believe that we are unworthy at a *foundational* level, not fit to connect with or to belong.

Shame strikes us at our core, leaving us convinced we're fundamentally flawed. No wonder we want to avoid shame at all costs!

Though everyone experiences shame, its triggers are extremely varied. What could be a minor embarrassment to one person could be a source of debilitating shame to another. Examining the differences between shame and other emotions such as embarrassment, humiliation and guilt further reveals why shame has such a profound effect on us. According to Brown, *embarrassment* is a fleeting feeling of self-consciousness or awkwardness— it subsides quickly. With embarrassment we know we're not the only one to have ever tripped on the stairs or forgotten a meeting, and it can even be funny. Not so with shame. Shame can last for years, it's isolating, and it pretty much stamps out the possibility of laughter. Meanwhile, *humiliation* occurs when we feel we don't deserve to be disgraced or shamed. Not so with shame. Part of the pain of shaming experiences is that we feel we deserve our shame. And finally, people often wonder about the difference between shame and guilt, and it's here that we circle back to the locus of self. *Guilt* is the feeling that results from an action we've failed at or failed to take, and it can actually be a healthy response. Not so with shame. Shame penetrates our very being—"I *am* bad" as opposed to guilt's "I *did* something bad." Guilt can help us change, while Brown's research reveals that shame "corrodes the very part of us that believes we are capable of change."[35]

No matter how you slice it, shame cuts deep, and it can affect every part of our lives. Unresolved shame can stop us from being the people we want to be and doing the things we want to do. But being freed from the lies we tell ourselves when we feel shame is profoundly transformative, and can give us the courage to be open, to be vulnerable, to be real, and to heal as we work through the deep hurts of life.

IDENTIFYING SHAME: NOT ENOUGH, TOO MUCH

With this theoretical framework of shame in place, let's get more concrete. I've found that in my own life and in my clients' experiences, shame often springs from the not enough/too much continuum. Take a look at the examples in the table on the next page and you'll see how shame often rises from the very common tendency to view ourselves as deficient or excessive in a particular area. In the blank spaces, you can jot down your own experiences of "not enough" and "too much."

NOT ENOUGH	TOO MUCH
I'm not smart enough.	I'm so smart people find me intimidating.
I'm not good enough as a parent.	I strive so hard to be a good mom/dad I'm a helicopter parent.
I can't let go of my children.	I secretly can't wait for my kids to move out.
I'm completely uninterested in sex.	My libido is so high there must be something wrong with me.
I don't have as much money as my friends.	I'm self-conscious about how well off we are.
I should be farther along in my career by now.	I should feel great for being a CEO, but now no one can relate to me.
I can never express myself well.	I always say too much.
I'm never satisfied with my appearance.	My beauty makes me self-conscious and intimidates others.

If you need help identifying the shame sources in your life, think about the last time you found yourself hiding, defending, or withdrawing in relationships. It is very likely that you were protecting yourself in these ways because of the fear that being seen as anything less than perfect or desirable would lead to certain disconnect with others. If you go back to the stories that opened this chapter, you can see what Brown calls the "unwanted identities" in all of them. These men and women feared being seen as hideous, incompetent, stupid, failing, imperfect, vulnerable... all identities that in our culture and our minds most assuredly engender criticism, rejection and disconnection. We are hard-wired for belonging, so any potential rejection from another threatens our need for love and belonging and will show us our sources of shame. You need look no further than the areas of your life where you feel an intense need to hide, defend, blame, or appease, and you will likely find lurking behind it your particular source of shame. A need to defend your parenting may show the shame you feel about not doing it "good enough." A need to hide your body with baggy clothes may expose your shame about your body. A need to inflate your work performance may indicate the shame that you are not being seen as competent. A need to hide your spending from your spouse may disclose your shame about not following your budget. A need to withhold parts of your story from those with whom you desire intimacy may reveal your shame that if they really knew you, they would not like you.

Recently I was helping my mother clean out her garage. In sifting through all the boxes I discovered she'd saved her calendars for years. My mother is an incredibly organized woman, and on her calendars she'd recorded birthdays, funerals, weddings, hair appointments, meetings—all of the things that were important to her—from big events to small.

"Mom," I said, "why have you been saving all these calendars?"

"Oh, I just thought one of you girls would want them some day," she said.

"Mom, nobody will need this stuff!" I said. "You should just pitch it all."

At the time I was knee-deep in boxes and focused on helping to get that garage spic and span, and I didn't think twice about our exchange or about tossing the calendars in the trash. But as I was driving back home to Des Moines from Texas it hit me: Very likely I'd caused my mother to feel shame. I felt guilty about how callous and "task oriented" I'd been and then I began to feel bad. Knowing all that I know about relationships, how could I have spoken to my own mother in a way that may have hurt her or made her feel badly? I was there to help her—and most likely I had hurt her instead.

Before I knew it, I felt so bad that my guilt (I *did* a bad thing) crossed over into shame (I *am* a bad person). I felt so much shame over how I spoke to my mom that instead of simply calling and apologizing for my hurtful remark I kept silent. Caught in the grip of my own shame, the situation felt too painful to talk about—even to make right a mistake I'd carelessly made.

That's what shame can do. It can take away your voice, and it can keep you isolated and afraid and paralyzed, shame-struck and stuck where you are. Allowed to proliferate unchecked, shame can eat away at the person you know yourself to be deep down. I like to think of myself as a loving, devoted daughter and a person who speaks and acts mindfully, but shame took my careless offhand remark (I did something wrong) and propelled it into the realm of my very selfhood (I am a bad person).

And if this kind of reaction can happen in the situation like the one I experienced with my mom, imagine what shame can do when it comes to complex issues such as body image, work and success, sex, parenting and family, and trauma. Again, think back to the examples at the beginning of the chapter. Shame prevented Bill from telling the truth about his job loss to his family, and kept him perpetuating an elaborate lie. Shame kept Suzy isolated and afraid of reaching out at the time when she most needed support. Shame over her perceived lack of wealth relative to her peers prevented Deborah from returning to the book club she very much wanted to join.

But is this the end of the story? Absolutely not! The first step in moving through shame constructively rather than letting it hold you fast in a place of pain is to recognize the sources of shame in your life. And that's exactly where Stop, Breathe, Believe can be a powerful tool in shining a light in all those dark corners that we really don't want others to see—and sometimes, don't even want to see ourselves. As we look more closely at the twelve categories of shame that emerged from the research of Dr. Brené Brown— Appearance and Body Image, Money and Work, Motherhood/Fatherhood, Family, Parenting, Mental and Physical Health, Addiction, Sex, Aging, Religion, Surviving Trauma and Being Stereotyped and Labeled[36]—we may find that we can identify with one or two categories in particular. That's where we'll learn more about shame in our own life story.

Remember that when working with shame, you don't have to get rid of it—instead, consider ways of learning to identify shame in your personal situations and work through it. Stop Breathe Believe can be a tool to help us *stop* and *recognize* the shame-based self-talk that is hijacking our brains from being able to respond to ourselves or to others in a way of empathy and compassion.

STOP BREATHE BELIEVE AND SHAME

One of the most powerful ways I personally use Stop Breathe Believe is as a means to recognize shame in my own life. *Stop* helps me to catch myself in a moment of shame and become aware of the shame story that's causing me to devalue myself. *Breathe* then helps me get re-centered through deep, relaxing breathing and a calm, clear moment in which I can take perspective of the situation and get a true look at what's going on. Then my *Believe* statement helps me recalibrate and come up with a healthier and more authentic story than the shaming story I was telling myself.

Shame!

On the 14-hour drive back to Des Moines from Texas I had plenty of time to think, and I caught myself replaying the moment I'd flippantly told my mom to "just pitch" the box of calendars, her box of memories.

"Okay, *stop*, Dianne!" I said to myself in the car. "*Stop*." To keep the negative, "beating myself up thoughts" at bay, however, I turned to Breathe. I took some deep breaths to calm my feelings of frustration with myself. It was while I was practicing Breathe that I identified the shame story that was at work. There were many threads of shame, but they all boiled down to one narrative: *I am a terrible daughter.* As soon as I saw that patently untrue story, relief washed over me. Of course that wasn't true! In fact it was ridiculous. Shame had been whispering a blatantly false story in my ear. But *Stop* arrested the swirl of negative thoughts, and then *Breathe* helped maintain that clear mental space in which I could discern the truth of what was actually happening. Then, with presence of mind restored, I offered myself these true statements that directly addressed shame's falsehood and affirmed the person I knew myself to be: "Dianne, you adore and respect your parents. You may have been insensitive, but you are NOT a bad daughter." Upon recognizing this, I came up with some belief statements that are true for me:

- You are a daughter who has great admiration and respect for your parents.
- Being present with Mom is one of the greatest gifts I can give her.
- Tenderness over tasks.

CHUTES AND LADDERS: A PROCESS TO UNDERSTAND SHAME

You may be wondering if it's just that easy. Especially if the source of your shame is one of those deep-seated, complex issues—an affair, a secret you've kept for years, an addiction, those feelings of not good enough or too much—you may be wondering how Stop Breathe Believe can help you identify and heal from the shame in your life.

The honest answer is: It's *not* that easy.

It's important to realize that understanding and addressing shame is a process, and processes take time. As with any process that occurs over time, you'll have up days, and you'll have down days. You'll have triumphs and you'll have setbacks. You'll make startling leaps forward, and some days you'll just feel confused and discouraged. All of this is okay—it's part of the process, and at any point along the way you're on your way to wholehearted living.

A metaphor that's proved helpful for many of my clients and for me is that of Chutes and Ladders™. Remember that classic childhood game? Land on a square with a ladder and you travel up, up, up and get ahead in the game. Land on a square with a chute, and whoosh, you slide down, down, down. But before you know it, with the spin of the dial you're back on a ladder and heading right back up. That's one of the wonderful things about chutes: There's *always* another ladder just around the bend! The chutes of life, while painful, are also invaluable sources of learning and growth. It's *all* part of the process of growing toward wholehearted living. The late Henri Nouwen offers wise counsel:

> When suddenly you seem to lose all you thought you had gained, do not despair. Your healing is not a straight line. You must expect setbacks and regressions. Don't say to yourself, 'All is lost. I have to start all over again.' This is not true. What you have gained, you have gained... When you return to the road, you return to the place where you left it, not to where you started.[37]

The metaphor of chutes and ladders applies to *any* process. Clients have described "falling down a chute" or "heading up the ladder" when it comes to weight loss, depression and bipolar disorder, relationship issues, divorce, trauma, learning a new skill or subject, starting a fitness program, physical rehabilitation, adoption issues, grief, and recovery from substance abuse and addiction. I'm sure the list could go on. One client now begins almost every session with a chutes and ladders comment. "Get ready, Dianne," she'll say, sitting down. "It's been a chutes kind of week."

Several of my clients have used a chutes and ladders illustration to create a timeline of their lives. As they ascend one of life's ladders, they identify high points such as education milestones, falling in love, marriage, the birth of children, landing a dream job, completing life goals, retirement, and special vacations. Then come times they fall down a chute. Low points include events such as divorce, death of loved ones, loss of a job, health crises, traumatic events, relationship struggles, or disappointments. Not only is this a useful way for me to learn the life events a client considers pivotal, but *a great many of those low points quickly reveal sources of shame.*

Chutes and ladders timelines can record the key events of an entire life, or you can easily make a chutes and ladders timeline for a single experience or short period of time. This has been enormously helpful in helping clients diagram and understand individual sources of shame. Suzy, for instance, made a chutes and ladders timeline that covered six months, beginning with her husband's trial. As she expected, it included many chutes: the newspaper coverage, a friend not returning her calls, a sneering look she got at the grocery store, an argument with her husband. But it revealed a few ladder moments that she'd understandably looked over in the midst of this tumultuous time: a supportive call from an acquaintance, a neighbor's offer to do lawn care, a heartfelt note from a friend she hadn't heard from in years.

By looking at her situation carefully through the chutes and ladders timeline, Suzy was able to identify her own triggers of shame. She could also then examine the self-talk associated with each of those shame triggers. One of her triggers was concern about what others would think. Here's the self-talk Suzy described in session: "People are going to reject me—who wants to be friends with a criminal's wife? People are going to judge me because my husband fooled others AND me. They'll think I am stupid for marrying someone who would do *this.*" It took a lot of courage to reach out and talk about her shame, and she was then able to identify the truth or the lie of her self-talk. Looking at her life through the chutes and ladders timeline helped her see that the painful tapestry of her experience was part of the process of life—the ups and the downs, the moments of shame as well as the moments of connection.

This exercise didn't eliminate shame from her life; instead it allowed her to become aware of and more resilient to shame by giving words to her hidden voice of shame. Shame is the secret keeper of our self-talk. Vulnerability is the key that unlocks the secret box.

Suzy relied on Stop Breathe Believe throughout the trial. She took her own image of a stoplight into the courtroom every day and kept it right beside her. She told me that she never even got to the green light on the card—she simply put her finger on the red light any time she felt fear taking over, and then moved her finger to the yellow light and breathed her way through the trial. "Just touching the card gave me a little bit of distraction from the steepest chute I've ever fallen down, and it kept me from going off into a panic of 'What ifs'," she said. "It helped me remember that with every chute a ladder follows, and that as painful as that time was, it brought about a silver lining: I learned who my truest friends were and I made new ones, too."

Shame is shame is shame. I have been privileged to become a Certified Daring Way Facilitator and Consultant (CDWF-C), and I teach classes on and provide consultations for Dr. Brené Brown's curriculum, The Daring Way: Show Up, Be Seen, Live Brave™. The Daring Way™ curriculum is a highly experiential methodology based on Dr. Brown's research that focuses on developing shame resilience skills and daily practices that transform the way we live, love, parent and lead.

One of the very best things about teaching shame resiliency workshops is watching the moment when the bonds of shame start to melt away for a participant. Suddenly, a person who's suffered in isolation for years from a private shame realizes that *she's not the only one.* Another realizes that the hidden quality he thought made him different and unacceptable is shared by many. Another begins to recognize that the huge fear of disconnection has the name of shame, and he learns ways to embrace and deal with the fear. It's one of the best feelings in the world, to know that *we are not alone,* and it's one of my most rewarding moments as a therapist when I have the privilege of witnessing shame's hold released from one more person. Engaging in the courageous act of being vulnerable and sharing our shame is one of the most radically transformative experiences a person can undergo. It's an exercise in mutual vulnerability, and it's healing for the person who's sharing as well as for everyone listening.

No matter how much training I've done and how much mindfulness I bring to my daily life, the chutes-and-ladders process of understanding and healing from shame is ongoing. Shame will always be with us. But we can learn to respond to it in new and more life-giving ways. And with deeper awareness of how shame is triggered within us, we're less apt to react out of shame and more likely to become aware of how we shame others.

Here is a list of belief statements that some of my clients have come up with in order to name their shame and heal from it:

- I am not alone in my shame.
- I am beginning to understand shame.
- My perceptions are windows into shame triggers.
- I am chosen.
- God is not ashamed of me.
- I feel empowered when I name shame.
- I am learning to reach out and ask for help when I need it.
- We all experience shame.

- I have to process shame.
- I am learning to manage shame in a new and different way.
- I believe I am important.
- I believe I have a valid opinion and it's okay to voice it.
- I'm learning a new tool to deal with shame.
- What I do does not define who I am.
- I'm learning that shame has been a part of most of my life.
- Who I am is enough.

BREAKING THE BONDS OF SHAME: MARK'S STORY

When I met Mark in 2010, he was a 34-year-old father of three whose residential construction business had folded in the wake of the 2008 economic collapse. He had tried in vain to find full-time work, but except for a bit of contract work here and there, he hadn't had steady employment in over a year. Behind on his mortgage, deeply discouraged, and with his temper often flaring out of control, Mark's wife Mallory had insisted he try counseling. Mark was very resistant to the idea of therapy, but he tried it and stuck with it despite his deep reservations, and what he learned surprised him. Here is his story:

"I built a great business in Des Moines and I really had no complaints about life until the end of '08, when the economy tanked and my business dried up just like *that*. I had some to get by on, but pretty soon I had to let my employees go one by one, and it killed me to do that. They've got families they're trying to provide for and I really felt for them, but I had no choice. In the end I had to shut everything down and sell off the equipment for whatever I could get. It was horrible—the most humiliating and frightening thing I've ever been through. I had to watch everything I'd built up over the years disappear before my eyes. I was powerless to do anything about it.

"I did not deal well with any of this. I couldn't sleep, and I just hated myself for losing the business and failing my family and my employees. Mallory had always wanted to stay home with the kids, and I wanted to be able to provide that for her. I cannot put into words the feeling of helplessness. I tried to find work but the whole construction industry was at a standstill at that point. We sold one of the cars, took the kids out of preschool, sold the gun collection I'd inherited from my dad, and did everything else we could think of to save money. Mallory got a teaching assistant job, but it was hardly enough. We started buying groceries on credit and got behind on our mortgage—something I thought would *never* happen to me in a million years—and it seemed like before I knew it we were in danger of losing it all. I don't think I'd cried since I was a little boy, but there were many nights I just broke down and cried.

"And on top of that, I was just *mad*. It was like a nightmare was happening in front of me, and I started to become this person I didn't want to be—every noise the kids made pissed me off, I was fighting with Mallory all the time, and then one night I was in such a rage I put my fist through a wall. That was when Mallory told me I needed to get some help, no matter what it cost.

"I'm sure you remember, Dianne, what a jerk I was at first. I had zero interest in being in therapy, and did not think I had problems big enough to be there. I think it was at least six weeks before I'd open up about anything at all, but I did start doing Stop Breathe Believe after our third meeting. The red thoughts I'd catch back then were all variations on the same theme: *I'm a failure; I'm the world's worst husband and dad; I've let everybody down*. It was really hard to get past those thoughts because I was *convinced* they were true, but I figured what did I have to lose, I'd try this Stop Breathe Believe thing and see what happened. The breathing part did make me feel calmer, and after I got better at it the deep breathing helped me sleep better, but I got hung up on the Believe part for a long time. I could come up with all sorts of great belief statements, but the problem was I didn't believe a one of them. If I tried to just say the opposite of a red thought, like 'I'm not a failure,' I didn't believe it for a minute. So my early belief statements were pretty generic, but I could live with those. I'd use ones like 'I'm learning things in counseling that will help' and 'I'm taking steps to help myself and my family'.

"It was when we did that chutes and ladders exercise on shame that everything started to shift for me. We mapped out all the chutes and ladders over the years, and obviously my biggest plunge was losing my business. I thought we were done, but then we mapped out all the *other* chutes that came from me losing the business, like my insomnia, my relationship with Mallory and the kids, my feelings of failure, etc. We talked about shame that day, and I remember I really resisted that for a while. I thought shame was when you'd done something awful and felt guilty about it, but after I learned about the difference between shame and guilt, it really rang true for me. I definitely had 'shame stories' going through my head all the time. *I am a failure. I am a terrible husband. I'm a pathetic excuse of a dad. You're not even a real man.* When I realized all those statements were being created by SHAME it brought me up short. Because really, they weren't even true. I'd had some unfortunate things happen to me and I'd made a few mistakes, but I also had years and years of being a great dad and husband and provider. When I saw how untrue these shame stories were it made me mad, but in a good way. I was determined not to go down due to a pack of lies I myself was making up because I felt so ashamed of not being a good provider or not being a "real" man. I felt really energized to turn things around. Even if I couldn't find a job, I would not let shame take down our family and all the good times we'd created together.

"I stuck with counseling for a while, and we continued to discuss shame. It was really eye opening for me. I realized that shame had actually been a part of my life even before I lost the business. A lot of the discipline I'd been raised with had been shame-based, and I didn't want to repeat that with my kids. But I also found out that I really didn't have to stick to such a rigid idea of what it means to be successful and a real man, either. I could let some of that old stuff go, the stuff that really wasn't working.

"Well, somehow or another we made it through. We did have to sell the house, but we're in a new place now, and Mallory is working on getting her teaching certificate. I patched lots of little jobs together until the economy started recovering, and now I'm partnered up with a guy and we have a new business. I still do Stop Breathe Believe, and in fact I relied on it just about every day when I was getting this second business off the ground—you can imagine how nervous I was. But when I start to feel uptight and jumpy, I stop what I'm doing and do Stop Breathe Believe to check in with myself and see what's up. Almost always, it's one of those shame stories going on. I use Stop Breathe Believe to see that story, calm myself down, and then immediately attack that lying shame story with the TRUTH. I'm really grateful for everything I learned, but most of all I'm grateful for my family and for everything we have. We got through all those dark days together, and we'll be together no matter what."

In Dr. Brené Brown's research, men tended to describe shame as failure, being wrong, being defective, showing fear, being criticized or ridiculed, and being seen as soft or weak, while women tended to describe shame as rejection, when others can see you failing, exposure, feeling like an outsider, and having their flaws revealed.[38] As you can see from Mark's story, a number of the typical shame sources for men were at work in him. He had not been aware that he was feeling shame until the chutes and ladders exercise revealed it to him, and then he used Stop Breathe Believe to continue identifying shame narratives and counteract them. The most present source of his shame was being unable to provide for his family, but that shame source was rooted deeply in the shame-heavy narrative with which he grew up: *You're not a real man/good husband/good father unless*.... Through the very good—and very challenging—work he did, he was able to see those unhelpful narratives and begin letting them go.

THE STRENGTH IN VULNERABILITY

When I have the courage to be vulnerable with others—about my sources of shame, my fears, my hopes, my intentions—I give others the courage to be vulnerable with me. One of the most poignant points that Brown teaches in her work on authenticity and vulnerability is that vulnerability is not weakness. It takes great strength and courage to be vulnerable enough to share our authentic selves with others, with all our flaws and gifts. As William James said, "It is only by risking ourselves from one hour to another that we live at all."

When we are able to lay down some of our defense mechanisms and the protective walls we put up to shield our hearts, we can pick up the practice of authenticity, and open ourselves to the possibility of greater community. My hope is that we will live life with the courage to be open and vulnerable and authentic with one another—in the chutes moments as well as the ladders—and that we can reach up and choose the ladders with hope of strength, community, and kindness.

BELIEF STATEMENTS FOR SHAME RESILIENCY

1. My limitations are my guidelines, not my stop signs.
2. We all experience shame.
3. Just enough is more than enough.
4. I am complex and vulnerable.
5. My instincts are designed to serve me well.
6. I may not have control over my circumstances, but I have control over my response to circumstances.
7. Life in all its ups and downs is a gift. ◀—
8. I am strong and able to face challenges.
9. I feel better when I can name shame.

AWARENESS MINES
EVERY RELATIONSHIP,
UNMASKS EVERY EVENT,
EVERY MOMENT,
FOR THE MEANING
THAT IS UNDER
THE MEANING OF IT.

Joan Chittister

8

The Mask and the Möbius Strip

Nearly every day, I wear a unique piece of jewelry. It's a simple silver bracelet with a twist—well, a half-twist. The bracelet, about half an inch wide, is flat all the way around, except for a half-twist that turns the bottom side up. But if you were to start at one point on the bracelet and trace your finger all the way around, it seems to have only one side, not two. In other words, it's a classic Möbius strip design.

If you want to create a simple Möbius strip for yourself, take a strip of paper and on one side write the word "inner," and on the other, write "outer." Give it a half-twist, and then tape the ends together to form a loop. Look how the inner flows into the outer and back again. That's a Möbius strip.

I wear my Möbius strip bracelet to remind myself that *I want to be the same on the outside as I am on the inside*. I want, in other words, to live my life with authenticity. To me that means I'm living out of my core truth—who I am at a deep level, independent of external ideas or pressures about who I *should* be. When I'm living with authenticity, I'm living out of my true spirit and ideals, and my actions and goals align with my values. I'm living with consistency between my inner and outer person. The Möbius strip, which appears to have two sides, actually has a single side. It's all of a piece. Whole. My bracelet is a visceral reminder of who I really am and how I want to live.

At first glance these desires may sound commonplace: Who *doesn't* want to be his or her authentic self? But living authentically is far more difficult than it sounds, and in fact, many of us hide our true selves, presenting a carefully tended mask to the world much of the time. It can be far easier and less risky to go along with the crowd, or blend into the background, or act in a way that's aimed to please others, especially authority figures or people we want to impress. Choosing authenticity can be a much harder path than we first realize.

Really, it's no wonder that so many of us put forward a mask at least part of the time. Life inevitably brings its share of hurt, disappointment, and disillusionment. If we risk vulnerability by putting our true selves out there and then that precious true self gets hurt, it's natural to want to retreat, to put up a protective barrier between your vulnerable, inner self and the outside world. In other cases, some of us are so reserved or perhaps unsure of ourselves that we act one way in public and only let our private selves emerge amongst a small, safe group of people. Some of us are fearful of criticism or judgment if we put our real selves on display, especially if our real self is unconventional or "socially unacceptable" in some way. Others find dissonance between their inner and outer selves as they strive to live up to an external set of rules and values—the *shoulds* and *have-tos* that we conform to in order to gain acceptance or approval. There are many, many reasons we could live out of a persona that obscures or conceals "the real me," many reasons why our inner and outer selves may not always align. The word "persona" comes from the masks actors wore in ancient Greek dramas. Most of the time the discordance between our persona or outer mask and our real, inner self comes from some well-intentioned, self-protecting reason, and it can be conscious or subconscious.

For delving deeper into a personal understanding of this concept it can be helpful to try an exercise that involves creating two masks. One mask represents the idealized outer person you present to the world—the ideal persona you want to portray. The other mask represents the true, inner self as it actually is—in all its shortcomings and strengths.

The masks can be as simple as two pieces of paper cut out to resemble a face; on one you jot down a list of "outer self" qualities, and on the other, the qualities of your inner self. Clients who enjoy expressing themselves through art have created beautiful plaster of Paris or clay masks decorated with paint, fabric swatches, feathers, glitter, magazine clippings, and ribbons. Others have decorated a plain mask purchased at a hobby or party store. Simple or elaborate, the purpose of the mask idea is to take time to reflect on what it is you want others to see, and what it is you don't want others to see and where those two things are out of alignment.

If you'd like to try the mask exercise for yourself, you can start with the simple paper and pen version. On one mask, write down all the qualities and attributes you strive to present to the world. What does your ideal outer mask look like? What do you want people to think about you? Examples might include: competent, attractive, intelligent, athletic, successful, good parent, kind, loyal friend, compassionate, generous, and confident. Be mindful as you contemplate and create your mask—give yourself some time to sift through any layers of self-protection you've accumulated over the years. It's simple enough to jot down a list of qualities, but the qualities need to be genuine.

♡ this exercise comes up so often w/ anxiety

For the second mask, even writing down how you see yourself may feel vulnerable. You'll need an ample helping of self-compassion. Be kind with yourself as you gently peel back the outer layers to find the inner, delicate layers of who you truly are. The inner mask is about interiority; it's about going deeper, past the best-effort veneer we put forth, and identifying some core truths about ourselves. Be intentional about stopping your mental chatter and getting in touch with your authentic self. I find that this takes some time, as almost all of us tend to be deeply invested in maintaining an idealized image that's acceptable and attractive to the world. Stop, take a deep breath, allow yourself to move past those idealized qualities you want to project, and sink deeper. It may very well be that many of your exterior qualities match up to your interior qualities. But for most of us, we'll find discrepancies and inconsistencies as we journey deeper.

PATRICK'S STORY: AUTHENTICITY IN CAREER

Here's an example of the outer mask and the inner mask from Patrick, a former client who at the time was a 46-year-old owner of a family business and contemplating a major career change:

Outer Mask: driven, in control, successful, smart, dedicated, go-getter, always informed, risk-taker, alpha male

Inner Mask: successful, smart, a regular Joe, self-doubting, worrier, short-tempered, easygoing, mild-mannered, feel like an imposter

It goes without saying that to be this honest and vulnerable takes a *lot* of courage. I've had plenty of clients who completed two very different sets of masks near the beginning of their therapeutic journeys and then many months or even years later into the process. It doesn't matter how long it takes. What matters is that you're committed to giving yourself—and the world—the gift of your authentic self, and that you're taking steps to get there.

Let me note that there's nothing wrong with wanting to put your best foot forward or to desire to be your best in public. It's a natural and healthy desire, and it's great to put forth your best efforts. But where we can get tripped up is the point at which our public personas and our private selves are miles apart. When this happens we're living far from our true inner core, and we eventually exhaust ourselves in trying to keep up a shiny façade that just isn't us.

Patrick had a good handle on who he was at his core as well on as the persona he was projecting. His public persona—the driven, risk-taking, alpha male—was an asset in the sense that it had helped him to become successful in business, and he relied on it to get through his days. But there was one big problem: Patrick was deeply unhappy. "Not *one* reason I took over the family business came from my true self," he said. "Not one." Family loyalty and a deep desire to please his father had convinced Patrick to continue the business after his father's retirement. He'd even adopted the "go getter" attitude of his dad in the way he ran the business, though internally, he was a mild-mannered, easygoing type of guy. "I figured I'd run it for a few years, just enough to tuck away a little nest egg and say I'd done my duty," Patrick said. "But one thing led to another and…well here I am, almost a quarter century later."

Twenty-five years may sound like a long time to live in a way that doesn't feel true or that doesn't seem to fit the real you. But remember that a great many people live out of a false self their entire lives, and for self-protective or even what they see as noble reasons. Patrick was motivated by a desire to do "the right thing." And he did do what he perceived to be the right thing—but for his father, not for himself. He had now reached a breaking point, and it was time to make sure his outer self was a truthful representation of his inner self, find some way to *choose* to live authentically out of his inner self on a daily basis.

That's a point that's worth emphasizing. Authenticity *is* a choice. It's not as if some lucky people are born with an inherent ability to be authentic and the rest of us aren't. Like so many things, authenticity is a practice, with all that word implies: a daily task, and you get better at it the more you do it. My Möbius strip bracelet is a much needed reminder that I have the power to choose to be authentic this very day, this very moment.

Being our authentic selves requires risk, and yes, sometimes we can get hurt. Patrick certainly found this to be the case as he made plans to sell the business and to venture into an entirely different career. His father was hurt and disappointed, and some of the customers who had been with the company for years took their business elsewhere. But Patrick rightly pointed out that the customers were "no longer my concern," and he felt confident that his dad would eventually understand why he had to choose a different path. "Dad's *starting* to get it," Patrick said, four months into his new career. "I'm so much happier and more relaxed now. I actually didn't realize how resentful and angry I'd become until I met this new, happier me. My wife was extremely worried at first—and I can't blame her, I was putting our financial security at risk—but she and the kids sure do like the real me a lot better, too."

RUTH: A BRIDGE BETWEEN INNER AND OUTER

The mask exercise can be a great way to lead us into the hidden issues that are holding us back from wholehearted living. Patrick came to therapy already aware of the chasm of difference between his inner self and outer self. Ruth, meanwhile, was so embroiled in painful emotions stemming from two hurtful experiences that she was unable to see the truth of her inner self. She described her experiences in writing.

"I met Dianne at a class she was facilitating and started counseling a few weeks later. It's a tough but wonderful experience and I feel like I'm finally putting ME back together!

"I started therapy after two failed friendships. My emotions were really raw, and I couldn't see my way through all the hurt and anger. I took to Stop Breathe Believe right away, because it helped me <u>calm down</u>, and helped me organize all the thoughts that were jumping around in my mind. Once I caught some of those thoughts, I paid attention to the ones that showed up over and over. Those were the thoughts that were tripping me up and triggering all that overwhelming emotion. So first of all, Stop Breathe Believe brought me some calm and some clarity. Instead of just flipping my lid and overreacting to the tiniest little thing, Stop Breathe Believe helped me slow down and become aware of thoughts that could very easily escalate into that storm of emotion. For example, some of the negative self-talk that Stop revealed was 'I'm not good enough' and 'I'll never have close friendships.' My failed friendships left me feeling that I wasn't good enough to be anyone's friend, and that I just wasn't cut out to be somebody's best friend. I was deeply self-critical and upset—and I was way too quick to assume that everything was my fault."

Good emphasis — sometimes we are a while here for — the process isn't all or nothing

"Sometimes, I was so upset that I wasn't able to get past the Breathe part—I just had to sit there and breathe to calm myself down. But as I continued to practice Stop Breathe Believe, I was able to turn my thoughts around. The belief statements I found most effective were 'I am a good and caring person' and 'I have several close relationships.' It's funny how when you're so upset you can't see the truth that's right in front of you. I DO have several good relationships, and just because a couple of friendships ended, it doesn't necessarily mean that others will.

"A little later on, Dianne and I did the mask exercise together. There was no question that my inside self and my outside self were at odds. When I first started therapy I was using a huge amount of energy to try and hide my hurt and anger and present a happy face to everyone—I didn't want to scare away any new potential friendships, and I wanted to convince myself that everything was fine. But that only worked up to a certain point, and I was working SO hard to convince everyone I was happy and not completely thrown by these failed friendships. So on my first mask, the face I wanted the world to see, I wrote 'sweet, kind, friendly, outgoing, loyal, genuine, funny.'

"For the inner mask, I took it home and did Stop Breathe Believe over several days before I was able to go down deep and identify who I really was. I needed to STOP and become aware of the real me, my true self as I perceived it then. And here's that person: afraid, livid, insecure, worried, loyal, needy. Obviously I couldn't even work on my issues without stopping to become aware of what they were. But seeing "loyal" show up on both masks was a real light bulb. It was because I was such a loyal person that having two friends turn their backs on me hurt so much. I'd gone out of my way for them and they betrayed me in return.

"The other thing the mask exercise helped me realize—and this was key for my healing—was that the inner mask I made then wasn't the permanent, core me. It was me in reaction to a terribly hurtful situation. I actually was many of those positive things I'd identified with the outer mask—but my overwhelming negative emotions and negative self-talk were temporarily obscuring the truth of who I really was. It was like I'd forgotten or lost the ability to see the real me. Seeing those two very different personas showed me how I'd lost myself, at least for a little while.

"From there, Stopping can help me re-find and re-mind me of my true self, and put myself back together. I still practice Stop Breathe Believe on a regular basis. When I start to feel self-doubt, I remind myself of the truth of who I really am, and I rely on the belief statement that I DO have good, close friendships, some of which have lasted for decades. I also shared with my husband exactly what I was feeling, and he opened up and told me about some of his own insecurities.

"The courage to let myself be seen exactly as I am, with my good and less than charming qualities, is an ongoing life goal. I'm still a work in progress, but I'm so much closer to authenticity and wholeness, and I'm starting to become excited to let my true self be seen!"

THE PROCESS OF BECOMING REAL = vulnerable

A huge part of our life's journey is coming to know who we really are, and day by day growing into that person. It's a process made up of daily choices, a beautiful, enriching growth experience that benefits our journey to wholeness and authenticity, and to integration and integrity. It's also a risky process. Putting our true selves out there is an act of vulnerability, and it puts us at risk for criticism and shame from others.

But it's absolutely worth the effort and even the pain. Allow yourself to imagine the possibility of *simply being you*, rather than pouring so much time and energy into projecting a persona of who you're "supposed" to be or organizing your life around living up to others' expectations. And if you're still wondering why you should risk rejection and why you should endure all the growing pains of becoming the real you, I have two answers for you. One is the obvious reason that you'll be happier, more energetic, and more fulfilled. The second is because the world needs your unique contribution. There are things you and only you can offer the world.

There's an amazing ripple effect that can happen when we live out of our *particular* truth and our own unique set of values and life experiences: We speak to the whole. Living out of our true self somehow, in a way that almost seems magical and some may call miraculous, touches a common place in us all. One person living authentically can inspire another to do so, and that person can inspire another, and so on and so forth, until we each give birth and give voice to the individual, real self that no one else in the world can.

In the beloved children's book *The Velveteen Rabbit*, the Skin Horse and the Rabbit discuss becoming real:

> "What is REAL?" asked the Rabbit one day, when they were lying side by side near the nursery fender, before Nana came to tidy the room. "Does it mean having things that buzz inside you and a stick-out handle?"
> "Real isn't how you are made," said the Skin Horse. "It's a thing that happens to you. When a child loves you for a long, long time not just

to play with, but REALLY loves you, then you become Real."

"Does it hurt?"

"Sometimes," said the Skin Horse, for he was always truthful. "When you are Real you don't mind being hurt."

"Does it happen all at once," he asked, "or bit by bit?"

"It doesn't happen all at once," said the Skin Horse. "You become. It takes a long time. That's why it doesn't happen to people who break easily, or have sharp edges or who have to be carefully kept. Generally, by the time you are Real, most of your hair has been loved off, and your eyes drop out and you get loose in the joints and very shabby. But those things don't matter at all, because once you are real you can't be ugly, except to people who don't understand."[39]

May each of us continue to grow into our real, authentic selves.

SOME GREEN THOUGHTS FOR GREATER AUTHENTICITY

1. Perfection is overrated. I want to be real. ← *yes! Sometimes, as a clinician, we get push back. I never wanted to be a therapist people couldn't relate to.*

2. I am growing steadily into authenticity.

3. I have a birthright of worthiness.

4. The world needs my unique voice.

5. My instincts are designed to serve me well.

6. What matters more than what others think of me is who I am.

7. I am fearfully and wonderfully made.

8. Vulnerability does not equal weakness.

9. I am learning to accept and express my true self.

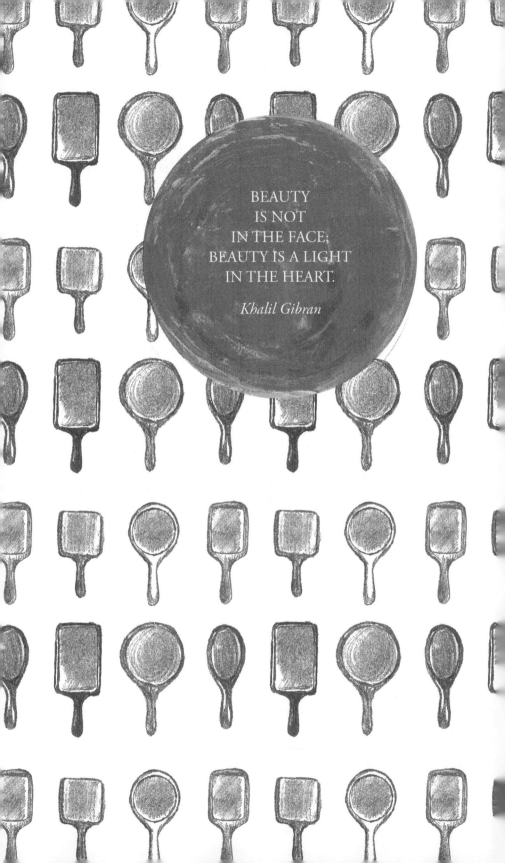

BEAUTY
IS NOT
IN THE FACE;
BEAUTY IS A LIGHT
IN THE HEART.

Khalil Gibran

9

Be.YOU.tiful

In late 2011 I traveled with our daughter Jill, a filmmaker, on a very special trip to Cincinnati, Ohio. Jill was making a documentary on autism[40], and in Cincinnati she would be interviewing Dr. Temple Grandin, the world-renowned author, speaker and autism expert who has autism herself. The whole experience was thrilling, but the highlight of my trip turned out to come from an unexpected source.

That same weekend there happened to be a conference for burn survivors in Cincinnati. On every street and in every restaurant and shop, Jill and I encountered people who had been disfigured by burns. The injuries I witnessed were profound and permanently life altering. Yet the people I saw were laughing and smiling and enjoying one another's company— appearance, at least for a time, was hardly a primary concern. I thought of what a vital community they had found at this conference, how liberating and comforting it must be not to be stared at because you're the only one who looks different. It was the *joy* I saw in their faces and not their appearance that caught and held my attention.

The experience was both eye-opening and heart-opening for me. Again, I lamented the overwhelming emphasis our culture places on external beauty—and such a narrow conception of what's considered beautiful at that. Snap judgments are made on the basis of appearance, and discrimination against people who don't meet the prevailing standard of beauty has been well documented.[41] Yet here before me was joy so palpable that I saw nothing less than beautiful in the faces and bodies of the burn survivors.

Sadly, it seems to take a wake-up call like this one to break through our ordinary cultural biases of what's considered beautiful and what's not. It's the rare person who's unaffected by the prevailing cultural notions of external beauty, and in fact it's far more common to be trapped by them. I have a client, for instance, who will not go to the grocery store if she has a zit. She's the magazine-cover epitome of what our culture tells us is beautiful: young, tall, curvy in all the right places, toothpaste-commercial teeth, shampoo-commercial hair. Yet she's become so dependent upon the affirmation she receives from her physical appearance that nothing less than perfection will do.

She's hardly alone. Most of us don't have the body of a supermodel like my client does, but how many times have we let our physical appearance stop us from doing what we want to do, or from being who we want to be? Have you ever turned down a social engagement because you're feeling overweight? Engaged in an extreme quick-loss diet in order to make it to the reunion, the wedding, the office holiday party? How many of us have ducked into another aisle if we run into an acquaintance on a bad hair day? How many of us feel like we can't run out to the post office without "our face" on? How many of us have spent more than we like to admit on beauty products or cosmetic surgeries?

How many? My guess is 99.9%! Nearly all of us, women and men, put time into enhancing our appearance, and certainly I count myself among them. In 2011, worldwide sales of beauty and personal care products totaled $426 billion,[42] and the financial web site Mint.com reports that American women spend an average of $15,000 on beauty products over the course of their lifetimes.[43] More alarmingly, a YWCA report on the consequences of beauty obsession on women and girls reports that over half of teenage girls have resorted to unhealthy means to lose weight, including smoking cigarettes, vomiting, skipping meals, fasting, and taking laxatives.[44]

There's nothing wrong with the desire to feel attractive and confident, nor is there anything wrong with taking reasonable measures to feel healthy and beautiful. But if girls who aren't even out of elementary school are starving themselves[45] to conform to what society considers beautiful, or if a healthy, attractive woman hides in her home until a blemish disappears, we've crossed into a danger zone. The problem occurs when we allow external beauty to determine our self-worth—even to the point of harming ourselves—and when we buy, quite literally, into the narrow prevailing cultural notions of what's considered beautiful.

Once again authenticity comes into play. When you encounter a person who's living out of his or her truest, deepest self, you know you've seen a beautiful person. Sure, the inner beauty is unquestionable, but have you noticed how they're attractive too, even if they don't have the face or the body that would earn them a place on the cover of a magazine?

What I'd like to offer you in this chapter is a chance to consider a new point of view when it comes to beauty. I won't be telling you to throw out your lipstick or stop coloring your hair or toss your high-end shaving cream. But let's consider what it might look like to discover and live out of an inner beauty that's so vibrant it becomes *outwardly visible*. Allow yourself to think about how liberating it would be to stop chasing after and suffering for false and often unattainable ideals, and instead be our *real*, beautiful selves. I'm under no illusions that it will be easy. The advertising industry and the fashion magazines do an outstanding job of convincing us that if we just buy more, apply more makeup, nip this and tuck that, work out harder, then beauty *and* happiness are ours.

But the advertising, fashion, fitness and beauty industries are in the business of selling products—they benefit directly from our collective low self-esteem. The real truth is that when you can access and express your inner, authentic and unique YOU, your real beauty shines through. You become be.YOU.tiful. Authentic, lasting beauty really has little to do with how we look. So instead of stopping at the surface—or letting the surface stop us—what if we learn to live wholeheartedly, offering the world the inimitable blend of gifts, talents, and beauty that is unique to each and every one of us?

If you're doubtful that this is possible, I don't blame you. It's difficult to overcome overwhelming cultural standards that daily make us question our true beauty. But there are plenty of people who are living out of their authentic, be.YOU.tiful selves, and they can help show us the way. We've already met a few: the hundreds of burn survivors who graced the Cincinnati streets with their presence, their joy, and yes, their undeniable beauty.

BEAUTY AND BROKENNESS

What I've witnessed time and again is how often beauty blooms directly out of brokenness. In this sense beauty isn't about physical perfection, but actually dependent upon those hard times and growing edges in our lives. It often takes a life-changing event to shake us out of the narrative that our culture feeds us about beauty.

One such story is from a client I'll affectionately call Pearl, because she taught me a great deal about the rich beauty that can result from significant sources of "friction." Pearl was diagnosed with breast cancer at the age of 32. She endured numerous medical procedures and chemotherapy and all the side effects her treatments entailed, but in the end a double mastectomy was necessary. She began counseling shortly after her diagnosis, and I was privileged to companion her through all the chutes and ladders experiences of chemo and surgery and the emotional turmoil that arose through any such life-changing journey. Pearl used Stop Breathe Believe as her daily situation called for to keep her spirits up during the tedious hours of receiving chemo, or to access a place of inner calm and confidence in the face of the inevitable fear that accompanies a frightening diagnosis. One belief statement she clung to will be familiar to anyone even casually acquainted with 12-step programs: "One day at a time." When things were at their worst, such as when Pearl was suffering acute nausea and painful mouth sores, it became "One hour at a time."

As you can imagine, it was a terrible blow to learn that she'd lose both her breasts, especially at such a young age. Concerned that a possible recurrence in cancer would be harder to detect with implants, she chose not to have immediate reconstruction. I'll never forget when Pearl dropped wearily into her seat several weeks post-surgery and said, "Well Dianne, now I'm bald *and* boobless," and then broke into sobs.

After several minutes of sitting with her through her tears Pearl suddenly blotted her face dry with a tissue and said, "I haven't been able to show Danny yet. I just can't. Honestly, I can barely even stand to look at myself in the mirror."

I asked her to tell me more about what she feared from her husband's reaction.

"Well that's just the thing," she said. "I *know* he'll be supportive and affirming and all that, but I'm still scared of being seen like this. It's not just the lack of breasts—it's the scars and the drainage tubes and everything. I'm a mess right now."

Pearl and I talked at great length about her fears of being seen. Slowly, over our next few sessions, we looked at those thoughts swirling about and identified the "repeat offenders" that bothered her most.

- I look and feel less feminine.
- I'm afraid Danny will find me repulsive.
- I'm afraid I'll find me repulsive.

Slowly Pearl learned to *sit with* these fears. Not try and banish them, not try and run from them, not try and ignore them. Being aware of our fears or other emotions and thoughts is different from dwelling on them in an unhealthy way. Pearl was taking an honest look at her *real* emotional landscape, and thus learning to deal with life-inhibiting thoughts in a way that helped her move forward and come to terms with her new normal.

Part of Pearl's work also involved an honest look at her outer landscape, her post-operative body. She did practice Stop Breathe Believe during this time, and the belief statement she used most often was "I know who I am and that hasn't changed." Gradually she became more comfortable with seeing herself in the mirror, but three months after the surgery she still hadn't let her husband Danny see her, and Danny was frustrated and hurt. "He's worried that I don't trust him enough," Pearl said. "I trust him completely, but I'm stuck here with these fears about my appearance. The worst part is that now it's not just about me but about Danny and our relationship."

Pearl also acknowledged that the longer she delayed revealing her body to Danny, the more frightened she became. She wanted to do something sooner rather than later, but said she wasn't yet ready to "rip the Band-Aid off all at once and go ta-da!"

It was Pearl who came up with an intermediate step that worked for her. She decided to ask her best friend Kirsten to look at her first. "She'll be the first non-medical person to see my chest," Pearl said. "I just feel like I need that before I show Danny."

The day Pearl told me about the experience of sharing herself in such a vulnerable way was unforgettable. She could barely get through the story for weeping, but her tears were tears of relief and happiness and of a burden beginning to lift.

"Kirsten was *amazing*," Pearl said. "One thousand percent supportive and affirming, in every way. We cried and cried together, which turned out to be healing for both of us. Kirsten told me all about how scared she'd been when I was sick. She said she'd never shared any of that with me because she wanted to be upbeat and positive for my sake, but she let it all out. By the end of the night 'the big reveal' was background news."

A few days after that, Pearl showed her post-operative body to her husband. "In lots of ways it was a repeat of the scene with Kirsten," she said. "Total support, total warmth, total acceptance. But of course there was a deeper level of intimacy with Danny. The way he looked at me… well somehow, without glossing over the fact that my body is permanently different, he made me feel beautiful and accepted. He saw through all of it, the scars and the flat chest and the *fear*, and saw the real me."

That day I received a potent reminder about the importance of being seen, *really seen*, exactly as we are. So many clients have sat in my office and wept over being ignored, not noticed, neglected or devalued in some way. At our best and maybe even especially at our worst, we all need someone who can give us the gift of seeing us, the real us, and loving us just as we are. Pearl had performed an amazingly courageous act in being vulnerable enough to expose her post-operative body. She was coming to terms with her new normal, and having the courage to let herself be seen was a huge step forward.

As the weeks progressed, the inner Pearl, the true self that had little if anything to do with external appearance, continued to flourish. In fact, Pearl would eventually say that she came to know her truest self, her inner heart, far better after the cancer and mastectomy and even because of it. Many people have had the experience of finding beauty through brokenness. This is a beauty that's birthed in our unique spirits, a beauty that's eternal.

Pearl's recovery didn't mean that she and her husband didn't mourn the loss of her breasts, and that she didn't have days when she felt "less feminine." Part of her journey to wholehearted recovery required grieving the loss of her former body, and learning to live with—and eventually love—her new body. Some days she wondered "Why me?" Some days she regretted not having reconstructive surgery at the time of her mastectomy, and some days she felt like "to hell with it, I'll just be flat." And some days she simply wanted her entire pre-cancer life back.

Pearl's journey is ongoing, and it will continue to have its share of tears and anger. She's still learning to let go of the image she'd held of herself, and the dreams associated with that version of Pearl. She had wanted to breastfeed her children, for instance. She and Danny had just started trying to conceive when she received her diagnosis. Now breastfeeding is out of the question, and it was heartbreaking to surrender that dream. She also had to let go of the image of herself as a voluptuous woman with a full C-cup, at least for the time being. But most difficult to part with was the idea that to be beautiful, a woman must have breasts, and better yet, full breasts.

"Honestly, most of the time I'm just glad to be alive," she said one day about seven months after the mastectomy. "But some days I just want my boobs back."

During that session, Pearl devised a new green statement: "I am SO much more than my breasts."

One of the avenues to healing for Pearl was becoming part of an online community of double mastectomy cancer survivors who elected to remain "breast-free." Pearl aptly described them as "beauty revolutionaries."

"Finding these women has been *huge* for me," she said. "They're so inspiring and so brave, and they showed me a new way to be in the world. They're completely unashamed of being flat, and proud of what they look like. Reconstruction is still an open question for me, but for now I'm learning to be okay as I am. I actually think *that's* the most important thing here. If I can learn to feel okay just like I am right now, flat-chested and scarred and my hair finally just growing in—then the rest is *nothing!*" Pearl laughed. "Seriously, most of all Danny and I are just grateful for my health—for our health. We know not to take that for granted now. And I've realized that the real me isn't dependent upon skin and tissue and fat. When you put it that way, it's not even close."

Pearl's double mastectomy is now two years in the past. She's still cancer-free, and she comes in to therapy every few months to check in. She's elected to forego breast reconstruction entirely. At a recent meeting I asked her to talk about how she came to this decision.

"Well, at first I didn't do the reconstruction because I was afraid," she said. "I was scared of the cancer coming back, and scared that implants would make the cancer difficult to detect. But as time went on and I got so much support from Danny and friends and family, and from you and my 'friends in the computer' that breasts just started to fade into the background.... What I mean is that my having breasts or not having breasts just wasn't such an issue any more. I realized that my self-worth does not come from any part of my body, and what makes me really attractive—like my sense of humor, my compassion for people, my intelligence—has *zilch* to do with breasts.

"The other thing, as you know, is that this whole crazy journey led me to a new career that I find *so* fulfilling. I *love* being able to be there for women and tell them with full honesty that I've been where they've been and that they can come through it and have a completely full and active life. Cancer doesn't have to stop you, and being breast-free doesn't have to stop you, either."

Pearl, an RN, now works in a radiology clinic and volunteers as a breast cancer patient advocate. She's also an active part of the online community that gave her so much support and companionship. She's found what she calls her "true calling," and now what she does aligns perfectly with who she *is*. That's authentic, be.YOU.tiful living.

It's worth reminding yourself that you are the only you there is—and that no one else who's lived in the past, present, or future will be able to make the contributions to the world that YOU are able to. As Eckhart Tolle put it in *The Power of Now*, "You are here to enable the divine purpose of the universe to unfold. That is how important you are!"[46]

And that is be.YOU.tiful. Identifying and living out your unique purpose is one of life's most important tasks, and is the source of true be.YOU.ty. "Beauty," writes John O'Donohue, "is the illumination of your soul."[47]

Pearl is living that be.YOU.tiful life. She knows exactly who she is and what she wants out of life—and what she wants to give to life. She's living fully out of her center. Her enthusiasm and vivaciousness are infectious and attractive—she embodies be.YOU.ty. She is fully alive and unreservedly sharing her true, be.YOU.tiful self with the world.

In Anne Lamott's wonderful memoir *Traveling Mercies*, Lamott recounts an experience of clothes-shopping with her best friend Pammy, who is dying of breast cancer. Modeling a dress for Pammy, Lamott asks if it makes her hips look big. "'Annie,' Pammy said, 'you really don't have that kind of time.'"[48]

That's right. *None of us has that kind of time*. Right now, let's *stop* allowing the ever-changing notions of ideal beauty affect us to the point that we feel ashamed of who we are and what we look like. Let's *stop* letting unattainable appearance ideals influence our thinking to the point that we take actions that harm ourselves. Let's *stop* curtailing our activities out of shame over our appearance. Instead, let's start a beauty revolution by taking a deep, health-giving *breath* and applying our energies to finding and living out of our real, be.YOU.tiful selves. Let's say no to the lie that the source of beauty is found on the surface—the perfect body, the flawless face, the immaculate home in the desired neighborhood, the latest model car, the "right" clothes with the "right" label. Let's not waste another minute on this kind of unhealthy thinking. Whoever you are, whatever you look like or feel like or act like, let's *believe* the truth that you are *already* beautiful, just as you are.

Anne Lamott's friend Pammy died just two weeks after giving Lamott the gift of such a powerful wake-up call. We really don't have the time to waste on the worries that stop us from being our true, be.YOU.tiful selves.

I've thought about the burn survivors many times since that weekend in Cincinnati, and the memory of their bravery and how they refused to let appearance preclude joy always inspires me. At some point I Googled the event, and discovered that the gathering was the annual meeting of the World Burn Congress, which is sponsored by the Phoenix Society for Burn Survivors. The Phoenix Society brings together burn survivors, their loved ones and caregivers, burn care professionals, and firefighters for a time of sharing stories and learning how better to support one another.[49] The society is named for the legendary mythological bird the phoenix, who is said to live 500 years or more, die in flames, and then rise from the ashes even more resplendent than before. The name perfectly captures what I saw on the streets of Cincinnati that day: be.YOU.tiful people who were be.YOU.tifully living a fresh chance at life.

May we all live each day as if newly risen. May you always be your true, be.YOU.tiful you.

BELIEF STATEMENTS TO INSPIRE BE.YOU.TIFUL LIVING

1. I refuse to be sold on an unrealistic idea of beauty.

2. Beauty is health, strength, and helping others.

3. When I am most authentic is when I am most beautiful.

4. I am a beauty revolutionary: I love me just as I am.

5. The wiser I become, the more beautiful I am.

6. I bless my own body and call it beautiful.

7. I am learning to see beauty in all its forms.

8. I choose to radiate love and hope and compassion—and that looks and feels like beauty.

9. I am learning to love my own unique beauty.

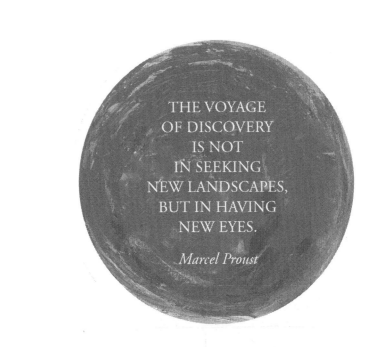

THE VOYAGE
OF DISCOVERY
IS NOT
IN SEEKING
NEW LANDSCAPES,
BUT IN HAVING
NEW EYES.

Marcel Proust

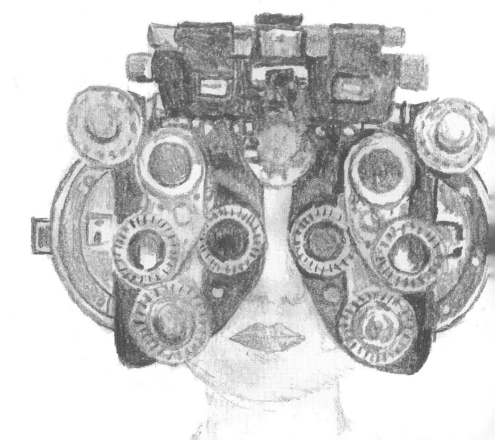

10

Perspectives and Filters

Rita and Jerry, an energetic, bright young couple in their late twenties, started couples counseling with me in their sixth year of marriage. They loved each other and had no plans to split up, Jerry told me, but they were fighting over "everything." From the way the dishes were loaded in the dishwasher to which kind of dog food to buy to how they wanted to spend their annual vacation. "We never used to be so *petty*," Jerry said with clear frustration. "Now I won't even dare buy a jar of peanut butter because I guarantee it'll be the wrong kind and Rita will jump all over me."

"Me?!" Rita interjected before I could get a word in. "I get scolded like a child if I put the wrong kind of gas in the car, or if I don't put *exactly* the right wording on an Evite, or God forbid if I want to *relax* and sit on the beach on my one week of vacation instead of climbing some mountain."

"Okay," I said, before Jerry could respond. "How about we start exploring what's underneath all this static?"

In the midst of conflict situations when we're feeling dug into our positions and emotions are running high, something like loading the dishes facing the silverware basket can feel like a matter of dire importance. But the reality is that whatever the surface issue, it's just "static" or noise obscuring—and symptomatic of—far more important underlying issues.

Over the weeks I spent with Rita and Jerry, I became very familiar with all their forms of "static." I won't bother to list them here—every one of us has our own version of static, whether it's with our partner or a close friend or a family member. Jerry was right—a lot of this stuff can be petty. But the conflict we're experiencing is not, and neither are the very big feelings that accompany any storm in a relationship. It's terribly stressful and heartbreaking to be in conflict with someone you love, and when these sources of tension go unresolved, relationships flounder or even rupture.

So while I did allow *some* time for Rita and Jerry to air their grievances, I didn't want the conversation to *remain* there. I asked Rita to tell me more about the conflict they were having about vacation. This can be one of those perennial sources of tension for couples.

"Well, I want to relax, and Jerry wants to hike Pikes Peak. And he makes me feel guilty and awful for not wanting to be adventurous and physical, like I'm lazy or something."

Jerry jumped in. "I've never once said you're lazy or—"

I held up my hand and Jerry fell silent as he realized he had interrupted. I reminded them of our ground rule to let each other speak without interruption.

"Well he may not have said it specifically," Rita continued, "but I can tell that's what he thinks. I work out all the time, and I don't want to spend my vacation doing strenuous exercise. I want to relax."

"And what are your thoughts on vacation, Jerry?" I inquired.

"I think the whole point of a vacation is to get to do things you normally can't do because you're at *work*," Jerry said. "I've always wanted to do Pikes Peak, and if we don't climb it now we may never do it."

"Can you tell me more about this sense of urgency?" I asked Jerry. "Why do you feel like you're running out of time?"

Jerry sighed. "Because Rita wants to get pregnant, like, yesterday, and once we have kids I feel like all our chances for adventurous stuff will be over. At least for a long time. I'm not ready to give up our current lifestyle. I think we should check some more things off our bucket list before we bring kids into the picture. But this has been such a *huge* fight that I finally agreed to Rita going off the Pill. That was maybe four or five months ago—we've been lucky so far."

"Lucky!" Rita said. "How can you say that? Five months and no pregnancy!" Rita turned to me. "I feel like we're running out of time," she said, her eyes growing misty. "What if there are infertility problems we didn't even know about? And I'm worried that Jerry will *never* be ready!"

"See?" Jerry said. "We can't get anywhere on this, because Rita gets hysterical and exaggerates everything. If you want my opinion, she's in a rush because lots of our close friends and both her sisters already have kids."

"Hey, I'm not the only one exaggerating," Rita said. "Just because we don't do Pikes Peak next week doesn't mean we'll *never* do it."

Let's pause the conversation right there and review everything that had come up within just a few minutes of talking. Already, an issue like where to spend vacation gave way to a much deeper, more life-altering decision like when, or even whether, to start a family. Clearly, Rita and Jerry had vastly different perspectives on this very critical issue. Rita wanted children immediately; Jerry wanted to wait. Rita wanted to start living a more settled, home-centered lifestyle; Jerry still wanted the freedoms of life without children. Rita saw family life as a new kind of adventure; Jerry viewed it as a hindrance to the kind of adventure he wanted. Rita wanted to ask her doctor about fertility treatments; Jerry wanted to "just wait and see what happens." Both felt as if they were running out of time, but for vastly different reasons. We could go on and on describing their different perspectives.

Whether you agree with Jerry or Rita or are indifferent to their situation, it's important to remember that differences in perspective aren't wrong and they aren't necessarily harmful. Everyone has a different perspective, and the diversity of opinions and viewpoints can be wonderfully enriching in a relationship (and in a family, a workplace, an organization, and so on). But *each person must put forth the effort to see the value in others' viewpoints.* In the case of Jerry and Rita, both were locked in to their positions, and both interpreted the other's perspective as a direct threat to their own. "Every viewpoint is a view from a point," writes Richard Rohr, "and we need to critique our own perspective if we are able to see and follow the truth."[50] It's only when we gain some self-awareness that we're able to critique our own dearly held viewpoint, and only when we can move toward understanding another's perspective that we can gain the empathy that allows a deeper understanding of each other's experiences and emotions. Part of empathy is perspective-taking, being able to see and understand what someone else is thinking.

Further complicating matters were the filters through which Jerry and Rita were arriving at and seeing his or her perspective. Filters are any of the factors that influence your particular perspective. Here are a couple of easy examples to illustrate the concept. If you recently experienced the breakup of a relationship due to infidelity, you'll naturally be more suspicious or more guarded when it comes to subsequent relationships. *Can I trust this person? Can I allow myself to be vulnerable again?* The experience of hurt and betrayal is the filter through which you may experience future relationships. In another example, if you grew up in a stable environment with caring parents who listened, you're far more apt to experience life through the filter of seeing the world as a secure place where happiness is possible.

Through time, healing practices, and *the power of our own choices*, we can change the impact of our filters as needed, and we can adjust our perspectives as needed. When we learn to become aware of the self-talk that arises from our filters, many times we realize that our self-talk simply isn't true. We can learn to re-write our self-talk, rather than live at the mercy of negative self-talk or the negative impacts of early experience.

So when clients start to learn about perspectives and filters and they worry that their filters are just too powerful or too entrenched to change ("I'll never stop clinging to people;" "Nothing I do will ever be good enough"), I'm happy to tell them nothing could be further from the truth. The potential to live into greater and greater freedom is limitless. My therapeutic practice and this book are founded on the truth that positive change is within everyone's grasp. Indeed, Stop Breathe Believe is based on the truth that becoming aware of the patterns of thinking that rise from our filters and that inform our perspectives is the first step in precipitating change. *Transformation is always possible.*

One tool that I often use to help clients become aware of the self-talk that's shaping their own perspective *and* see and become more empathetic toward others' perspectives is called the Feedback Format®, designed by Pia Mellody. Here's how it works, in brief.[51] In response to an event that caused discord between you and another person, respond to the following prompts:

Feedback Format

1. Describe the event as an objective reporter would, just the facts.
2. The story I am telling myself is...
3. I am feeling...
4. What I need from you is...

I often have used my Feedback Format responses to formulate and write a letter to someone in order to understand my own perspective more clearly. The letter does not have to be sent; it can be a tool for understanding one's self—one's own motives, reactions and responses. When we can become aware of *the story we're telling ourselves*, we can realize what's fueling our own emotions; often, we discover that the "issues" are our own. In addition, it's immensely helpful to recognize what it is we want or need from another—sometimes we don't even know until we take the time to listen to ourselves.

In addition, the Feedback Format is a fantastic tool for living in relationship with others. In community, our relational life can get complicated. This tool is an integral way to look at and begin to understand another's perspective. It can help clarify what's "my part" and what's "your part" in a relational struggle, which can help us take responsibility for our behaviors.

As Jerry and Rita continued in therapy, I learned more about the filters that were leading them to their perspectives on starting a family. Rita did indeed feel motivated to start a family sooner rather than later because her close friends and two younger sisters already had children. She felt left out of her peer group—or as she put it, "not part of the mommy club." And now that five months had passed with no pregnancy, she was worried about infertility. In addition to all of those concerns, she certainly did not feel heard by Jerry.

Jerry, on the other hand, felt the longer they waited, the more mature they'd be and the more money they'd have saved up, and the more chances they'd have for spontaneous adventures. Those were his practical considerations. But his emotional motivations were more powerful. His father had died of a heart attack at the age of 47, and Jerry felt that overwork and stress were direct contributors to his father's poor health and premature death. Given this incredibly powerful filter, it made sense that Jerry wanted to get in as much fun time away from work as he could, and as soon as he could.

Both Rita and Jerry had blind spots in their thinking. That's simply what happens when we're caught in the grip of red self-talk that's obscuring the reality of a situation. Moreover, when we insist on our own position, we're unable to entertain or sometimes even see the other person's perspective. Both Rita and Jerry had to realize that the other's perspective was as valid as their own. In Rita's case, she needed to hear and empathize with Jerry's real fears about mortality and his desire to enjoy life, and she needed more information in order to know if her worries about infertility were justified. In Jerry's case, he needed to hear and empathize with Rita's very valid points that the risks with pregnancy and the incidence of infertility rise with age. This couple had to learn to listen and really *hear* each other. David Augsburger, author of numerous books on counseling, conflict and relationships, says that "Being heard is so close to being loved that for the average person, they are almost indistinguishable."[52] We underestimate the profound power of simply being heard, of having another person give us the gift of their attention. And while the fact that Rita's friends and relatives had children had little bearing on his own perspective, Jerry had to come to realize that it held a great deal of emotional weight for Rita. Each needed to try to become aware of and appreciate the other's perspective, as well as the filters that were influencing their perspectives.

During our sessions, I often employed the two-minute hourglass with Jerry and Rita. The hurt they were both feeling was powerful, and not only did they tend to interrupt each other, making true dialogue impossible, the built-in pause gave them time to descend past reactionary responses and move closer to the heart of the matter. With this built-in pause, they were able to respond rather than react. I encouraged them to buy a two-minute hourglass and use it at home as well, even if it felt awkward or contrived. I've found that many of us need to re-learn how to incorporate silence into our daily lives and our conversations. This may especially be the case in homes where tension runs high and fighting is frequent. We often don't know how much we're missing silence and respectful dialogue until we bring more pauses into our daily life and give ourselves a chance to truly hear the other person, to linger, to listen.

Jerry and Rita also practiced Stop Breathe Believe. After doing Stop Breathe Believe individually and finding it useful, they came up with an innovative way to use it. They practiced Stop Breathe Believe *together* if a conversation escalated into an argument. This was a great way to put the brakes on a hurtful conversation, release the tension of an argument, and come together to move forward in a positive direction. Once again, it gave them time and space in which to respond rather than react—and it actively involved them in doing something *together*.

Here are some of the belief statements Jerry and Rita used most often during the initial 3-4 months of counseling:

Jerry's Belief Statements:

- I am willing to try speaking less and listening more.
- My father's story is not my story.
- Parenting is its own kind of adventure.
- Absolutes like "never" are rarely true.

Rita's Belief Statements:

- I am willing to try speaking less and listening more.
- Comparison is the seed of discontent.
- I'm excited about living MY story.
- The more wisdom I gain, the better equipped I'll be as a mother.

Belief Statements as a Couple:

- We want to learn to hear and listen to each other's perspectives.
- We love each other no matter what.
- We're willing to go deeper and get to the heart of the matter.
- We're married to the person with whom we want to spend the rest of our lives.

A few months into therapy, I asked Rita to describe what Stop Breathe Believe looked like when she and Jerry practiced it together.

"Well, when a discussion starts to heat up, whoever gets a hold of themselves first will say, 'Okay, let's stop this,' or just 'Stop,'" she said. "We agreed beforehand that no matter how angry we were we'd stop and regain our bearings. Then for Breathe, we use our two-minute hourglass and close our eyes and take deep breaths until the time's up. We're always calmer after that, and coming up with a belief statement we both like has actually been kind of fun."

"Except for that time we *couldn't* agree on a belief statement," added Jerry, grinning.

Rita started to giggle. "That's right—one time we actually got in a fight over which belief statement to use—*Let's try this again or We love each other no matter what*! But then we realized how ridiculous we were being, and we got so cracked up we laughed till we cried."

Through learning to appreciate and empathize with each other's perspectives, and then finding a way to engage in respectful conversation together, Jerry and Rita were learning to *build bridges* rather than *drive wedges*. This is an analogy I often use with clients experiencing any type of relationship conflict. Can we find a way to build a bridge between each other, even if we have radically opposing viewpoints, or is this issue going to drive a wedge between us? A green statement many of my couples clients use is, "Let's face the situation *in front* of us rather than let it be a problem *between* us."

The issue of when to start a family was a wedge that was steadily driving Jerry and Rita apart, but what they learned in therapy and through the use of Stop Breathe Believe was a bridge. Laughter was a huge bridge for Jerry and Rita. So was doing Stop Breathe Believe together. So was the simple act of using a two-minute hourglass to bring pauses into their critical conversations. So was discussing the filters that were coloring their individual perspectives. All of these are bridge-building—and thus relationship-building—activities.

As we continued to work together, Jerry and Rita worked their way through some pivotal moments and some tough issues. A turning point for Rita arrived when she was able to understand the filter of what she called "Jerry's hurry-up-and-go" thinking.

"Of course I knew his dad died young," she said one afternoon. "But I just wasn't connecting it to his drive to do more and more, and do it *now*. And I definitely wasn't connecting it to the Pikes Peak trip specifically. But now I understand it's all of a piece, that even if he wasn't consciously thinking about his dad when it came to Pikes, it's in his mind somewhere and it's all connected. Getting that missing piece made me have a lot more empathy for Jerry. And a lot more patience."

"Ditto on the empathy part," Jerry said. "It's true I don't have baby fever like Rita does, but if a bunch of my buddies got together and say, did a hiking trip without inviting me, I'd feel left out. I know it's not a perfect analogy, but putting it in terms like that got me out of my head and more into Rita's."

In other words, by better understanding each other's filters, Jerry and Rita were better able to entertain and understand each other's perspectives. They learned how to listen to each other, to appreciate each other's perspective rather than view it as a threat. They learned to let the other person speak, and to wait a sufficient period of time before replying, so as to respond rather than react. And they learned to use Stop Breathe Believe to examine their own thinking and appreciate the thinking of their spouse, and to draw closer together.

Overall, they learned the idea of "us-ness" and seeing past their individual positions—no matter how different their perspectives—rather than the narrow vision of "me vs. you."

BELIEF STATEMENTS FOR EXPANSIVENESS OF VISION

1. I am learning to appreciate other points of view.

2. Understanding others' perspectives enables me to be truly helpful.

3. I choose to listen for the benefit of others.

4. I am learning to see reality for what it is.

5. Fully understanding one person's viewpoint is more than enough.

6. Other viewpoints are not threats to my own.

7. I am learning to be judicious in hearing all perspectives.

8. I am learning to become vulnerable and let others take control from time to time.

9. I'm growing into naming and claiming my unique perspective.

THERE IS
A CRACK
IN EVERYTHING.
THAT'S HOW
THE LIGHT
GETS IN.

Leonard Cohen

11

The Crack in Everything

"Sometimes, it seems like tragedy is a just a matter of staying tuned."

These haunting words came from a client who lost her only child to a sudden illness. Sadly, experiences like hers are not as rare as we would like. Tragedies and traumatic events are headlining stories in our 24-hour news cycle; it seems not a day goes by that we don't hear of large-scale tragedies such as war, natural disasters, violent crime, acts of terror, or horrific accidents. In our own communities we all have friends and family members who've endured some kind of trauma or deep grief. The very day I began drafting this chapter, my local newspaper covered stories of a man who'd accidentally shot and killed his daughter, a young man who died when he was pinned between a truck and a semitrailer, a tropical storm making landfall in Mexico, a couple whose baby died of a gunshot wound during a domestic dispute, and the sudden death of an actor in the prime of his life.

My client is heartbreakingly right. Sometimes it does seem like tragedy is just a matter of staying tuned.

Trauma and tragedy occur every day. Most of the time it's to those anonymous folks in the news we'll never know, but sometimes it arrives on our own doorstep. These moments of deep, searing pain may not garner headlines, but they're no less painful. The death of a loved one. The dreaded diagnosis. A son or daughter who gets in serious trouble. The loss of a home. The end of a significant relationship. Exposure to violence or abuse, whether isolated or chronic. The experience of war, whether as a combatant or as a civilian back home, waiting for a service person to return. A loved one with a chronic disability.

If you can picture life's challenges on a spectrum, with the minor irritations on one side and significant stresses somewhere in the middle, we now find ourselves at the other extreme, in the realm of tragedy and trauma and deep grief.

When we undergo a traumatic event or are working through deep grief, we're best served by a variety of support systems. Whether it's Stop Breathe Believe, therapy, prayer, taking solace in nature, medication, exercise, talking with family and friends, attending support groups, meditation, or any combination thereof, dealing with trauma is not something to be done alone. Saying yes to help is a courageous and necessary act.

As for Stop Breathe Believe, it's no accident that the technique mirrors our natural healing process. Any time deep pain occurs, we *stop* and regroup, we rely on some means of *steady support* to get us through, and eventually, although we're forever changed, we *believe* in life again.

Stopping after a deeply painful event, especially when it arrives as a shock, is so very important. It's actually a built-in part of our recovery process. Statements like "I just can't believe it" or "I stopped functioning" or "I feel disconnected from everything" or "I'm numb" all point to the temporary paralysis that occurs when terrible things happen unexpectedly. This is the mind's natural way of helping us process trauma. If at first we don't feel the pain—just as a jolt of adrenaline can numb the body after a physical trauma—this is fine. Our job is simply to stop. The reality will hit us sooner or later, when our mind is ready to begin allowing it in.

Psychologically, stopping gives us time to adjust to a new and deeply unwelcome reality. It allows this new reality to sink in, to be accepted as fact. This is a healthy response. We need to give ourselves the gift of time—the gift of stopping. It's no wonder we're unable to think, or work, or parent, or eat, or make decisions, or do much of anything after the death of a loved one or the end of a cherished relationship or a cataclysmic event such as a natural disaster. The need to stop is programmed into our psyches and into our bodies. It's also worth noting that if we *don't* stop—if we try to bypass grief in the form of overwork, overeating, over-exercising, or any other form of avoidance—our bodies will often stop for us. We get sick, or we have panic attacks or dissociative episodes, or we sleep excessively. These are all well documented responses to shock and grief.

Then, eventually, we can come back to the breath. Of course we've been breathing all along, but during the period of shock and readjustment our breath may be the last thing we notice. In the wake of a tragedy it may feel like life can't go on—and we may not want it to. One of the biggest frustrations for people in trauma is that the world *does* goes on—how can people just keep working and having fun when it feels like our whole world has just collapsed? But the constancy of the breath is a visceral sign that life persists. Following the breath—giving our attention to the present moment, even if it's a pain-filled moment—brings mindful awareness to our new reality so we can begin integrating it into our lives. This is when acceptance of that new and unwelcome reality begins to occur. Moreover, we can count on slow, deep breathing to bring us increased calm. Deep, abdominal breathing is so effective in bringing relaxation to the body and equanimity to the mind that it's being taught in VA hospitals around the country to help returning soldiers recover from PTSD.[53]

"Just breathing" may be all we can manage for quite some time, and this is perfectly okay. Bringing mindful attention to the breath and engaging in a daily breathing practice can keep us centered and carry us along.[54] The flow of life continues, and it will be waiting for us to step back in fully when we're ready. This in fact may be the hardest part—saying yes, choosing life in spite of.

But that's where belief comes in. While stopping is necessary in the early days after a tragedy and breathing can be used at any time in the healing process for relief, belief is the sustaining force that will carry us through the years. Finding a belief statement and a belief system in which we can put our full confidence gives us the kind of foundation we need for going forward after a deeply traumatic event. Moving forward at this point may feel like no more than putting one foot in front of the other. That is perfectly okay. Taking refuge in our core beliefs can provide a sense of security at precisely the time when life seems unstable, and a sense of meaning when our experiences of deepest anguish make life seem senseless. For some people, belief encompasses religion or spirituality. For others it's a belief in human goodness in spite of acts that strike us as evil or immoral. For some, it's a belief in the resiliency of the human spirit. For others it's a belief in the outreach and support of the community. Belief anchors us, grounds us, and points the way forward to live beyond whatever circumstances assail us.

STOP BREATHE BELIEVE AS A LONG-TERM COPING STRATEGY: KIM'S STORY[55]

Kim, a dietician at a private clinic, and her husband Trey, a civil engineer, were close friends with another couple, Melissa and Allen. The foursome, all in their mid-thirties, had been friends since high school. Between them they had five children, and the two families frequently spent time together and had vacationed together several times. Kim and Melissa were best friends, as were Trey and Allen. Each couple's children considered the other couple their aunt and uncle.

Over nearly two decades of friendship there had been only one major source of contention between the four friends, and it was Allen's incessant texting. As Kim recounted, at first it was "no big deal." They'd all purchased smartphones at about the same time, and according to Kim, "we *all* texted and played with our phones like crazy, especially at first." But soon the novelty wore off for everyone except Allen. Kim knew that Melissa was frustrated with the frequency of Allen's texting and web surfing, and that it had been the source of heated arguments. "Even Trey, who's as laidback a guy as you'll ever meet," Kim said, "got impatient with Allen. You just couldn't get him away from that phone. But Allen had always been a gadget guy and we figured he'd eventually come around."

But if anything, Allen's texting increased. "He wouldn't even put the phone down in the middle of a conversation," Kim said. Kim and Trey tried to overlook what by then they assumed was a full-blown "addiction," but they drew the line at Allen texting while driving. "That one was a non-negotiable," she said, "especially since my kids were in the car with Melissa and Allen at least once a week."

Soon enough everyone—Melissa, Trey, Kim, and even the kids—were after Allen to stop texting and checking his email when he was behind the wheel. "Allen had some near-misses when he was distracted," Kim said, "running stop signs and stuff, and one fender bender. But he kept insisting we were overreacting. But finally Trey and I put our foot down and said our kids couldn't ride with him any more. I think that was the first time Allen realized how serious we were."

Here Kim began to weep. She reached for some tissues and paused to compose herself. I remember this part of the session very clearly because of the dread I could feel, even though I knew what was coming.

"It was two weeks later that I got the phone call," Kim said. "At first I couldn't even process what I was hearing…I thought there was some huge mistake. It was Melissa's sister on the phone. Allen was in the hospital, and Melissa and Katie, their daughter—were gone."

Driving back from a family trip to the movies, Allen lost control of the car while distracted with his phone. He drove through a divider and hit a tree; the passenger side of the car took most of the impact. Melissa and eleven-year-old Katie died at the scene. David, Melissa and Allen's son, escaped with minor bruising, and Allen was being treated for a concussion, lacerations, and broken ribs.

Needless to say, both families were devastated, and my client Kim was left to deal with layers upon layers of trauma. In addition to the shock and pain of losing her best friend and a little girl she loved as much as her own, all of her closest circle of friends and family—Trey, Allen, her own children, and David, the surviving son—were traumatized and bereaved. The story was picked up by the local news, and not only did reporters cover the funeral, Kim would come home to find news crews parked in front of her house. In all the stress and the grief, friction arose between Kim and her husband, and then there was the inevitable anger Kim felt toward Allen. Melissa and Katie had died in an entirely preventable accident, and for months everyone had pleaded with Allen to stop texting while driving.

"You just can't imagine how horrible it was," Kim said. "No one who hasn't been through something like this can possibly get it. My best friend and her child were gone and I felt like I had to 'stay strong' through it all for my kids, and for Trey, too, who was a total mess. He and Allen had been friends almost as long as Melissa and I had, and he wanted to help Allen, but he was also so mad at Allen at one point he said he wished it was Allen who'd died. Honest to God, Dianne, I felt that way too! I couldn't help it. This was just so...so stupid and irresponsible and unnecessary! And the kids...you can't imagine how heartbroken they were. I couldn't even bear to look at them at the funeral...it took all I had not to start screaming in the middle of the service."

When I met Kim, Melissa and Katie's deaths were only 4 ½ months in the past, so the trauma and the grief were still quite fresh. She was still angry at Allen, but that had faded somewhat; she said she felt sorry for him for what he'd been through. He'd lost his wife and had a son in deep grief, he was facing criminal charges for involuntary manslaughter, he had enormous legal fees, and the guilt he felt was unbearable. He'd even spoken to Trey about suicide.

"But now, Allen won't speak to us any more," Kim said. "He's isolating himself and won't really speak to anybody, but Trey and me especially. I do get it—I'm sure we remind him of Melissa, and he probably feels a hundred times worse when he sees us."

After noting that Kim was reporting on everyone but herself, I asked her how she was doing and how she'd been feeling over the past few months.

She shrugged. "Well, that's part of why I'm here," she said. "I handled the whole thing by staying busy. I took care of the kids, supported Trey...

and I threw myself into doing something that would honor Melissa. I set up a college fund for David, along with a campaign to raise awareness about the risks of texting while driving. If it was up to me this would *never* happen again to *anybody*."

Kim had used every spare moment to work on the fundraiser. "I've been on a crusade," she told me. "I'm determined to use this horrible, horrible hurt in some positive way. I spend pretty much every waking moment on it, even at work."

Busying yourself after a traumatic event is a fairly common response. Grieving clients have described putting in extra hours at work or the gym, becoming consumed with funeral arrangements and estate settling, or taking on a project, such as Kim had done. In her case, she'd launched the fundraiser and awareness campaign while still working full-time. Her efforts had been recognized in the local papers, and she'd received lots of praise and affirmation. She'd raised a great deal of money (and had also given a significant amount of her own), and she said she'd found "at least *some* healing" through her efforts. She started therapy as the fundraiser was winding down.

"I recognize that I still need help in processing everything," she said. "But to be perfectly honest, the main reason I'm here is that when the fundraiser's done there's going to be this great big void—and I'm terrified of what's going to show up there."

I commended Kim for her self-awareness and asked her to tell me more about her fear.

"Well, all the busy, frantic stuff will be over," she said, "and I'm going to be left with…well, after all of this is over, all I've got to do is *just live*."

Kim may not have known it at the time, but there was deep wisdom in that statement. After the loss of someone dear to us, we're all faced with the task of *just living*. We have to carry on without our dear ones, and it can feel absolutely impossible. Oftentimes in trauma, breathing becomes the goal. Just to take a breath can feel like a struggle.

Breathe seemed to be the most important initial segment of Stop Breathe Believe for Kim. She needed immediate relief, and she needed a coping skill to take home and rely on. We did several breathing exercises together, and at that very early stage, we came up with a single belief statement she could hang onto until our next session: *I am learning a new coping skill that will help.*

As our time together progressed, I instructed Kim in how to capture some of her red thoughts, and as we examined them we realized that they all boiled down to one overarching worry that she'd presented early on:

This was me

"I'm afraid about having free time." Often, busyness can distract us from the loss. But Kim was fully aware that the grieving she needed to do had been pushed aside, deferred. She was afraid she wouldn't be able to do it alone. I assured her that I'd be there to walk through it with her, and that she could rely on Stop Breathe Believe along with her other coping tools to navigate this difficult landscape of trauma and deep grief.

Kim came up with a number of belief statements to address that big, scary red thought—*I'm afraid about having free time*—that held her in its grip.

- I'll have more play time with my children.
- I'll have more "me" time.
- I'll be able to rejoin my book club.
- I'm looking forward to some financial relief.
- I'll get to spend some more time with Trey.
- I can start planning a family vacation and look forward to that.

I continued to see Kim on a weekly basis as the fundraiser came to a close, and for eight months after that. She did not have it easy. At times she described having a rush of emotions bearing down on her; sometimes it felt like she was "reliving Melissa and Katie's deaths all over again." I assured her that this reaction was perfectly normal and that she could also expect a resurgence of difficult emotions on significant dates, such as the anniversary of Melissa's death, her birthday, or when Allen's case went to trial. We also discussed the unexpected moments of grief that can pop up, usually when something reminds us of our loved one. Kim had one of those moments when a person in line at the bank mentioned the last movie she and Melissa had seen together. "I ran out of the bank," she said, "but then I sat in my car and did Stop Breathe Believe until I calmed down and was able to go back in."

As Kim was a "do-er," she enthusiastically practiced Stop Breathe Believe on a daily basis, and she taught it to Trey as well. "At first, I used it like a life raft," she said. "For a while it felt like I was literally going to die of grief. I missed Melissa so much, and thinking of Katie gone at just 11 years old made the whole universe seem unjust and awful. I'd catch myself slipping down this black hole, and I'd use Stop Breathe Believe to bring myself back. It was times like that that I'd need to get very quiet and focus so I could identify the one negative thought that was sending me into no-man's land. It was very important to focus on one thought—otherwise it was just too overwhelming. It also gave me confidence to know that I could take on one thing at a time. Then I'd take as many deep breaths as

I needed to stop shaking, and I'd answer that red thought with a belief statement. If my red thought was the fear of 'I'm not going to recover from this,' I'd answer it with a green statement like 'I've come to know who my support system is' or 'I am stronger than I ever realized' or just 'One day at a time'."

Another part of the healing process for Kim has been writing. "Studies have suggested," Daniel Siegel writes in *Mindsight*, "that simply writing down our account of a challenging experience can lower physiological reactivity and increase our sense of well-being, even if we never show what we've written to anyone else."[56] Letter writing or keeping a journal are excellent coping skills. They help us stop and pay attention to our feelings. In Kim's case, she'd numbed herself with running hard and fast. Stopping to write in longhand revealed what she'd blocked out, and she sometimes used a Feelings List (see Appendix I on page 182) for help. When the feelings were big and bold and ugly—she encountered plenty of rage at Allen, for instance—she counted it as good work. Journaling or writing letters never intended to be sent is an excellent means for feeling emotions and expressing sentiments that could be harmful said aloud.

Some people prefer to keep their letters and review them from time to time to see their progress. Others burn them to cleanse and let go, and that's what Kim chose. The emotion didn't simply disappear after the letter was destroyed, but she found the symbolism of the act very healing. Kim was doing something important in *choosing* to let go of these emotions. Letting go isn't a one-time event—it's something that must be committed to and carried out multiple times—but it is predicated upon a decision. Making the decision to let go even a little bit can give us a sense of control when life feels out of control. It reminds us that we're *active* participants in life when it feels like life is being done to us.

The important thing is to make a plan to process the emotions and the pain. Having a plan can give us a sense of security. A plan might include checking in regularly with a friend, doing therapy, or meeting with others who are grieving.

When Kim finds herself assailed with negative emotion, whether it's anger, deep grief, or resentment, she uses Stop Breathe Believe "to reorient" herself. "Stop Breathe Believe, especially after I practiced it for a while and came to trust that I could rely on it, usually got me over the hump, whatever it was," she said. "It was the little bit of a pause I needed to regroup and then keep going, and to remind myself that there was another moment on the way, an all new moment, and that I could *choose* to make that moment better."

Kim understands the chutes and ladders nature of healing from tragedy. But she has reliable tools, including Stop Breathe Believe, her letters, and a strong support system in her extended family and in Trey. The awful experience of shared grief has even brought them closer together. Kim described a "shorthand of grief" she shares with Trey. "I don't have to try and explain and explain how awful this is—he gets it. We get each other, and sometimes we just hold each other and cry." In his poignant book *Out of Solitude,* Henri Nouwen beautifully captured the precious gift of a loved one who can be present with us in our hour of greatest need.

> When we honestly ask ourselves which person in our lives mean the most to us, we often find that it is those who, instead of giving advice, solutions, or cures, have chosen rather to share our pain and touch our wounds with a warm and tender hand. The friend who can be silent with us in a moment of despair or confusion, who can stay with us in an hour of grief and bereavement, who can tolerate not knowing, not curing, not healing and face with us the reality of our powerlessness, that is a friend who cares.[57]

Kim is still sad, and *some* degree of sadness will always be with her, but she's no longer helpless before that "no man's land" of grief. She's gathered enough strength and support to move forward, and to help others in a healthy way.

"My whole life took on an entirely new perspective after the accident," Kim wrote. "I lost my best friend and Trey lost his best friend. But Trey and I are so profoundly grateful for each other and our family. We parent differently now, and our relationship is different, too. We're way more honest with each other, and more empathetic all around. We make a practice of being grateful every single day, even for the tiniest things. Lastly, I've learned how to help other people without exhausting myself. I am better at keeping boundaries in place and make sure I'm spending time with the people I love. I'm not going to waste another minute or take another minute for granted."

There may be no more transformative experiences than trauma and deep grief. "Breaking point" moments can hurt like nothing else, and they irrevocably change us. But *if we choose to allow it,* they can also break us *open,* catalyzing tremendous growth that we never would have experienced otherwise. We *do* have the power to make personal choices that are more life affirming and healing for ourselves and our loved ones, and with support systems in place, it *is* possible to recover from devastating experiences. The cracks in life—they're everywhere and they're unavoidable. But each and every one offers a new and incomparable source of transformative light.

BELIEF STATEMENTS FOR BREAKING POINT MOMENTS

1. The cracks are how the light gets in.

2. Letting others take care of me is perfectly okay.

3. It's okay for me to stop doing and just be for a time.

4. I'm learning a healthy way to deal with overwhelming emotions.

5. I can trust my built-in processes for healing.

6. I can count on deep, abdominal breathing to help me find calm and focus.

7. I'm learning to give myself the gift of stopping.

8. I'm developing a new kind of strong.

9. I'm learning to ask for help without feeling bad about it.

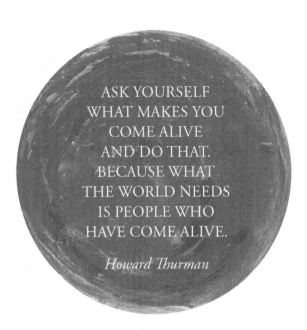

ASK YOURSELF
WHAT MAKES YOU
COME ALIVE
AND DO THAT.
BECAUSE WHAT
THE WORLD NEEDS
IS PEOPLE WHO
HAVE COME ALIVE.

Howard Thurman

12
Fully Alive

Years ago my friend Nawal began periodically asking me when I felt most fully alive. Nawal is a spiritual person and a deep thinker, and I always appreciate her perspective. But many times I didn't know how to respond to her question.

Of course, that was half the point. Questions that require some time for pondering are so often the best questions. When I had a chance to reflect, I found that I had different answers to the question according to different points in my life. As a young mother, for instance, I would've felt most fully alive cuddling my babies or witnessing their first smiles, steps, and words. As a graduate student it would've been one of those *aha* moments when a professor imparted just the insight I needed, or when all the research came together and I arrived at an insight on my own. Fully alive moments at this point in my life include the everyday moments of sharing life with Roger, significant conversations with Justin and Jill and Brent, witnessing clients break free of what's keeping them from wholehearted living, outdoor activities such as snow skiing, backpacking, and walking, and moments of solitude when I'm deeply aware of the Divine.

The times when I don't have a ready answer to Nawal's wonderful question are just as revealing. When I find myself disconnected from what makes me feel most fully alive, it's because I've temporarily gone off track and need to get back to my center in order to rediscover what brings me life. Anything can knock us off center for a time. Grief, a major transition, illness, mental or physical fatigue, an argument or misunderstanding with loved ones, unexpected events, excessive busyness, or even positive events that jar our routine can unsettle our sense of stability or purpose. For me, remaining in touch with who I really am and what leads me into full, abundant life requires a daily practice of sitting still and allowing the breath of God to flow freely through me. I need to intentionally allow the space and time to tune in and cultivate awareness. It takes silence to hear those quiet nudges that are so often the voice of our deepest self and of the Divine. And it takes time to sink past all the other mental chatter in the funnel that's obscuring that still, small voice that's always there, always guiding us. As a matter of fact, sometimes when we do slow down, the mental chatter can actually feel like it's getting louder because we are not accustomed to being still long enough to listen to it.

What is it that allows you to slow down and be aware of when you are most fully alive? Any practice that enables you to listen to your deepest self will work. I have one client who gets up fifteen minutes earlier than her family so she can drink a cup of coffee in solitude and check in with herself. During that quiet time she sets an intention to be open to whatever may be next for her and follow any nudges that steer her toward full life. Several clients say that being in nature gets them in touch with their authentic selves and makes them feel fully alive, and that's certainly true for Roger and me. Another client tinkers with his car engine in the garage each evening to "get things in perspective." For others it's running or hiking, a meditation practice, yoga, taking long drives, golf, gardening, spending time with pets, cooking, or an artistic pursuit. These practices are acts of self-care and awareness that support full, wholehearted life.

Ultimately, Nawal's thought-provoking question taught me not only to pay attention to what makes me feel fully alive, but to pay attention to the times I don't have an answer—to this question or *any* question. If I'm aware of what makes me feel fully alive, I celebrate the deep rightness of living out of my center and take the time to be grateful. And if I can't at that moment identify what makes me feel fully alive, I treat it as an opportunity to *live the question*. Instead of fretting that I don't have an answer, I'm grateful for the cue that I need to practice Stop Breathe Believe and get re-centered. Living that question is like Stop Breathe Believe writ large: not knowing what makes me feel fully alive is my signal to stop my activities, get centered through some breath practice and deep listening, and then set my intention to *live toward* that place of full aliveness.

It may take time to arrive at an answer that feels authentic. But that's okay. Often, not having an answer to the question has taught me more than I would have learned otherwise. My intention now is simply to *live the question* until the time is ripe for knowledge. I trust the process and life lived with awareness to lead me to the answers I need. This well-known quote from 19th century German poet Rainer Maria Rilke states it beautifully:

> ...try to love the questions themselves, as if they were rooms yet to enter or books written in a foreign language. Don't dig for answers that can't be given you yet: you live them now. For everything must be lived. Live the questions now, perhaps then, someday, you will gradually, without noticing, live into the answer.[58]

I now try to make a conscious choice each day—despite how vulnerable it feels—to live with hands open wide, heart receptive to change and to the flow of life, and feet steady on a path of being willing to be "in process" rather than in a position of knowing all the answers. I am trying to *love* the questions and *live* the questions so as to be able to *live into* an answer when the time is right.

And how do I know that I'm living into a life-giving answer—or even that I'm living the right questions? Believe me, I don't always know! But through my practice of non-judgment I've learned not to become discouraged when I go off track, and simply to pick myself up and begin again. For me, part of what's required to be fully alive is that on a consistent basis, I open up to examine my thoughts, feelings, and behaviors and then take the time to determine which ones I want to embrace and which I want to let go of. This is where the practice of mindfulness, prayer and Stop Breathe Believe come into play. To be fully alive, I know that I can't get stuck in unhealthy thinking or fall prey to self-defeating thoughts. Stop Breathe Believe helps me to become aware of my thoughts, feelings, and ideas, take the time with deep breathing to be intentional about my choices, and then actively choose to direct my thoughts, feelings, and ideas toward healthy, life-giving thinking. If I'm practicing awareness and intentionally living out of my deepest self, I'm more able to live the questions that lead me toward full, abundant life.

Struggling with implementing the process of Stop Breathe Believe is normal. One of the most frustrating things for me is when I *know* that something would be good for me—like exercising more regularly or drinking more water—and I *still* don't do it. At these times, it is crucial to remember to give ourselves grace, and to recognize that we're learning something new and to be kind with ourselves.

Sometimes I find that a simple breath practice helps align my intentions with my actions. For instance, on those days when my schedule is packed and it seems it will be a race to the finish all day long, a simple mantra aligned with my breath—*Inhale peace; exhale hurry*—gets me re-centered and mindful. With that simple practice I'm actively embracing peace, and letting go of that sense of frantic hurry. Being in a state of hurry drains me of life and energy, whereas cultivating peace always leads me to life. Another crucial life-giving practice for me is that on a daily basis, as much as I'm able I direct my thoughts to beauty, which for me means seeing God in everything, even if it's just a glimmer of divine light. From the dew on the leaf as I'm walking in the mornings to the tears on a client's face; from the red-winged blackbirds singing out their dawn chorus to the flat tire that invites help from a stranger; from the taste of a fresh garden tomato to the sand dropping through the hourglass. The element of choice is key here. Rather than become discouraged over the inexorable progression of time, or become angry or afraid over the flat tire, I can choose to find the element of beauty hidden there.

It's not always easy. Sometimes we can feel as if the tears will never end; often it feels like time is getting away from us; sometimes no kind stranger shows up to help us with whatever flat tire (literally or figuratively) life throws our way. But how much more life-giving it is to search for and find something beautiful, however small, rather than become stuck in life-draining pessimism. For me, it is much more *fun* to live the question of "Where is the beauty here?" and to search for the message of life in a circumstance or a challenge. Sometimes the beauty may be someone standing alongside you in a really tough spot. Sometimes the beauty may be in someone's empathetic response like, "Wow, the situation you're in really sucks right now." One of the gifts of the practice of Stop Breathe Believe for me has been the deep belief that even life's quietest or toughest moments can reflect the Divine and carry the potential to lead me to full, abundant life.

And once you're in the habit of *expecting* moments of life-giving beauty, you'll find them in the most unexpected of places. I had one such experience recently when I was teaching a laughter yoga class at an assisted living facility. Laughter yoga requires you to let go of any pretensions and any concerns about how you look. In fact, the sillier you look and feel, the better. That said, I'd never actually *seen* myself in the midst of a laughter yoga session until that day at the assisted living facility. On one side of the fitness room was a wall of windows that offered a beautiful view of the surrounding grounds and gardens. On the other was a solid wall of mirrors. In every other gym I've been in people stood facing the mirrors to watch themselves work out. But the assisted living residents had their priorities right: They wanted the view of nature. Which for better or worse, left me staring at myself in that wall of mirrors.

Well, it was no time to succumb to self-consciousness. Throughout the session I was very intentional in making eye contact with the participants, and giving myself over fully to the laughter and release of a good laughter yoga session. However, at times I couldn't help catching a glimpse of myself teaching, laughing, and leading. It was a bit of an out-of-body experience to glance up at the mirror and catch myself doubled over in a fit of laughter. What an experience of not only being fully absorbed in doing what I love, but of observing myself in the act of doing what I love. It was as if I was given quick, mini-snapshots of myself in a moment when I felt fully alive. What a powerful visual, to be witness to myself in a moment of full vitality.

It got me thinking, *What if?* What if there were mirrors, literal or otherwise, that could provide a glimpse of ourselves absorbed in a moment of full aliveness? What would it look like for me? What would such a mirror reflect for you? Holding a child or grandchild? Belting out a show tune in the shower? Creating a work of art? Sharing a significant conversation around the dinner table with family or friends? Engaging in prayer? Skiing the slopes of freshly fallen snow with loved ones? A night of camping in the woods? Dancing with abandon? Taking a leisurely walk with no set destination? Cheering on your favorite team to victory? Reading a book that gives words to an experience you haven't been able to articulate? Savoring a delicious meal? Realizing you're not alone?

When are we secure enough and engaged enough to feel fully alive? When is it that we simultaneously love what we're doing and love who we are? Not just in the extraordinary moments, but in the ordinary. William James wrote, "Seek out that particular mental attribute which makes you feel most deeply and vitally alive, along with which comes the inner voice which says, 'This is the real me,' and when you have found that attitude, follow it."[59] What fantastic counsel! How would it be to experience moments of full aliveness *each and every day?* How would it be to *dwell* in a sense of being fully alive?

Some of you will know immediately what makes you feel fully alive. For others, it will take some time to discern the answer. That's perfectly fine. Half the fun is in living the questions. And living your own questions is an invaluable learning process. One helpful way to think of what fully alive would look like for you is to think about what fills you up rather than drains you. What restores you, energizes you, enriches you? Identify those life-giving activities and attitudes and follow them.

Or maybe you're in a place where coming at the question from the other direction makes more sense: What drains you, saps your energy, makes you feel fatigued and unenthusiastic? It might be big issues such as financial challenges or relationship problems or a health crisis. These are big drains, things that sap our life energy swiftly. But it's also worth remembering that the little leaks or drips, while not as quick or dramatic, have the same effect in the long run. Think of the energy we waste in worrying about getting the email just perfect, or waiting to make a call until we've figured out exactly what to say, or the feeling of going through 10 outfits each morning, or the chances to speak up that we let pass by. Over time, the slow leaks and drips are just as significant as the sudden, large drains—and could be more insidious because often, they deplete our energy without our awareness. But once you can identify the leaks and drains and recognize them for what they are, you're far better equipped to deal with them.

Another good thought-provoking exercise is to ask others when they sense that you're most fully alive. It's fascinating to hear others' responses, and to see how their perceptions coincide (or not) with what you perceive of yourself. It's another opportunity to see if your inner self is aligning with your outer self. And sometimes, others are able to see gifts and abilities in us that we're not yet able to. When one client asked her thirteen-year-old son when he thought she was most fully alive, he thought for a minute and said, "When you're on the phone with Aunt Sue." Sue, my client's younger sister, was going through a very painful divorce. My client was always worried that she wasn't doing enough to help, or wasn't saying the right thing. But her son's perception that she was *fully alive* during those tough conversations convinced her that something important was happening, that she was indeed giving something worthwhile. "And you know," she said, "I thought about that for a long time, and I realized that's one thing I've always been good at—I'm a good listener. I was always so focused on not being able to say the perfect thing that would solve Sue's problems that I forgot how powerful it is just to have someone give you their full attention. I really *like* paying attention with my whole self, and I'm not as uncomfortable with the silence any more."

In the therapeutic context, no matter the challenges the client is facing, asking the question "When do you feel most fully alive?" is often a conversation stopper—in the best possible way. My clients know that I am not afraid of silence. I intentionally promote silence so that we can ponder our answers rather than rush to a quick response.

For many of us, all this talk of full aliveness may seem utterly foreign. Many of us can't consider looking for intense experiences of vitality—we're just hopeful for the wherewithal to get out of bed and to participate in life again. There are times when almost everything may feel draining. Eating regularly, washing our hair, answering email, making it to an appointment…it all requires monumental energy. This is where we can start small and look for ordinary moments that will turn our gaze toward vitality and hope. We can celebrate any positive, life-affirming step, such as complying with a medication regimen, participating in a social activity, noticing beauty, or leaning on a belief statement and breath practice to get through the tough moments. At times it's going to be a long, slow process to being able to feel fully alive. It is courageous and wonderful to stay committed to getting better when it feels so much easier to give up. In these moments the belief statement of "I CAN make choices to live more fully" is huge. Our belief statement can affirm our personal autonomy and remind us that hope is very real. Just that little bit of light can lead us on and keep us actively moving, or at least looking, forward.

The gift of being fully alive can turn up in the midst of the ordinary, the painful, the joyous, the extraordinary, the silence, the unexpected. Watch for it. It is beautiful.

BELIEF STATEMENTS FOR FULL, ABUNDANT LIVING

1. I can gently let go of moments of self-judgment.

2. I'm discovering the richness of simply being alive.

3. I'm committed to living out of my deepest, truest self.

4. The ordinary is extraordinary.

5. I don't have to have all the answers in order to live full, abundant life.

6. I'm learning to love *living the questions.*

7. I choose to live in awe of the wonder of being alive.

8. We're created for community and connection.

9. I am learning to be fully present to myself and my unspoken desires.

EPILOGUE
A Prayer For Connection

You, the reader, my new friend, you are not alone. Many times during our life journey we may think we are the only one struggling with a particular situation or frustration. May this book assure you that you are not alone in the struggle, in the journey for truth, for clarity, for understanding, for wholehearted living, for living fully alive. As you are able to give words to your struggle, may you be able to share your story with someone who has earned the right to hear it and hold it.

We are created for connection—with all of the parts of ourselves to be whole, with others in community, and with our understanding of the Divine. May your life be filled with touch points of caring and compassion with yourself and with others.

As you and I are stumbling through life—messing up, getting up and trying again—may Stop Breathe Believe be a tool that you will join me in using. May it become a part of your story that helps you connect, and grow in depth, wisdom, and love.

My hope and prayer is that Stop Breathe Believe is a tool for inner transformation for you—not just information, but transformation.

The change, the transformation, the journey…
stop and allow yourself to be more aware of your thoughts;
breathe deeply and become more present to yourself and your world;
and *believe* the green thoughts that empower your most authentic YOU.

May your journey to wholehearted living be rich and deep and wide. Namaste. May the Divine in me touch the Divine in you.

Gratitude

Counseling, envisioning, being encouraged, drafting, researching, feeling vulnerable, writing, being excited, editing, teaching, revising, re-writing, having courage, designing, being scared, praying over, being encouraged some more, crying, persevering, feeling grateful, proofreading, waiting, pressing send and feeling *very* vulnerable, then being where we are today, with you holding this book in your hand…awe. Creating the book you are reading was truly a collaborative effort, and there are a number of people I'd like to thank for their part in this incredible labor of love.

First, I am just so grateful to God—for life and breath and joy and struggle and all of the amazing people that You have created. What a privilege of getting to do life together with God. Thank you.

To my clients: You inspired me to create Stop Breathe Believe and you continue to inspire me on a daily basis. Your courage and vulnerability and strength in the face of adversity motivate, encourage, and humble me. As you know, I think each one of you is precious, *truly* precious, like a valuable, priceless jewel.

I could not have written this book without the steadfast love and support of my husband, Roger, who has read every version of every page. Roger, you are the most amazing soul mate and friend I could *ever* dream of. Your love for me is stunning—beautiful. I love you and I thank you.

To our son Justin and our daughter Jill and her boyfriend, Brent: Your love and support have encouraged me. You each exemplify qualities that awe me; I truly love and respect each of you. Our trips and short breaks together and laughter and phone calls along the way were monumental in the "we can do it" category. Your edits, input and curiosity about Stop

Breathe Believe are invaluable. I often felt and heard the "Go, Mom, go!" from each of you.

My parents, George and Gena Morris, have weaved unconditional love, support, and encouragement into every fiber of my life for all these years. I am beyond grateful for your love and your care.

Wanda and Hershel, Roger's parents, have poured into me as if I was one of their own. Hershel passed away in 2011 and we all still miss Papa immensely. Meme, you are one brave girl! Thanks for your love.

To my precious extended family, I cherish each one of you: Melinda, Gary, Tracy, Katy, Greg, Annette, Jeff, Lane, Joni, Alanna, Beau, Rhonda, Brent, Kailee, Damian, Thomas, Samuel, Clint, Grant, Jim, Martha, Jacob, Savannah, Zach, Rebekah, Don, Cy, Bobby, Sammie, Tommy, Sue and the rest of the gang.

To Helen: Thank you for allowing me to share a piece of your story. You are an inspiration to me and to so many others.

To Adele VerSteeg, thank you for helping us understand the Enneagram in a Stop Breathe Believe way!

To the Family Legacy office: What a treasure to share my everyday work world with each of you—Ed, Pat, Nancy, Deb, Joel, Cindy, Kristin, Sarah, Jenise, Michelle, Dave, Kim, Gary, Tonja, Holly and Jana.

To my small group friends, the community that has laughed, cried, prayed, discussed and sculpted our lives into being through the years: for Sharon, David, De, Ron, Marianne, Greg, Scott, Michelle and Jon; for Brenda, Pat, Cindy, Aaron, Dana, Walt, Cheryl, Kelley and Lisa; for Arlyne, Dave, Lori, Bill, Barb, Magdi and Nawal.

To other encouragers along the way: Donna, Marcia, Dave, Helen, Dena, Laurie, Debra, Jane, Kristie, Sally, Lisa, Donny, Susan, Kathy, Lou Ann, Kirk, Barb, Gary, Bonnie, Terry, Sharon, Angie, Nena, Tim, Brenna, Mary, Randy, Alicia, Marshall, Cheryl, Tom, Jean and Kelly.

To the Son Foundation, thank you for your encouragement and belief in this work.

To my readers, on whom I officially have RDD, Reader Dependency Disorder. I have needed you and depended on you and I thank you: Donald, Dick, Terry, Murdoch, Robert, David, Robyn, Ronda, Monica, Nancy, Nawal, Jill, Justin and Roger.

To Brené, Robert, Murdoch, Barrett and all of the team at The Daring Way™, a huge thank you—you who are changing lives by dumping out one shame bucket at a time. May the life of the whole world be daring and may the marble jar revolution continue. Each one of you is amazing!

To Nancy and Nawal and Kathy: Thank you for your curiosity, the listening, the picking me up and the holding me up during the stumbling moments of the "everyday struggles and joys" of the book birthing process. Your support has been life giving.

To Alanna: Your artwork is beautiful—thank you for sharing it with my clients the last five years and on page 16 and the original for page 108 and your stoplight on the bottom right of page 187. May your creativity take you far!

To Bess Yontz: Your artwork for my website is gorgeous. May others find your work as amazing as I do. Thank you.

To Robert: Thank you for accepting our request to paint a stoplight so many years ago! We are thrilled to share your art on the cover. Your art is captivating!

To Lori: We were all thrilled the day you said yes to helping us tell the world about Stop Breathe Believe.

To Brit and Sarah: Thank you for your patience and enthusiasm in helping me learn the social media world.

To Monica: We kept dreaming of what this would look like and it is happening—thank you, my friend. You are so talented and so gifted. Your drawings for the beginning of each chapter capture your creative skill. I am so glad you said yes to Stop Breathe Believe.

To Catherine: The interviews about client stories, the laughter, our Southern accents, the hours on end around the kitchen table and the couch with the fireplace going—you are a genius! Your writing and your ability to say what I *meant* to say and *wanted* to say are amazing. I did a cartwheel (well, almost a cartwheel) the day you said yes to Stop Breathe Believe. Catherine, I am so grateful that during the process of writing Stop Breathe Believe, not only were you the editor extraordinaire, but you also became a cherished friend.

Finally, to my readers: Thank you. May you discover a more generous and daring you, a you who lives the questions and follows your desires, each and every day, every hour, with every thought you choose.

Appendices

APPENDIX I: THE FEELINGS LIST

able
abnormal
accepted
accomplished
affectionate
afraid
aggressive
alive
alone
ambivalent
amused
angry
annoyed
anxious
apathetic
apologetic
appreciated
apprehensive
arrogant
ashamed
aware
awe
awesome
awful
awkward
bad
beautiful
behind
best
better
betrayed
bewildered
bitter
blah
bleak
blessed
blissful
blue

bored
brave
broken
calm
capable
cared for
caring
cautious
certain
cheerful
cherished
childish
close
clueless
cold
comfortable
compelled
competent
complete
concerned
confident
confused
contemptuous
content
cool
courageous
crabby
crappy
crazy
creative
critical
crushed
curious
dangerous
daring
dead
defeated
dejected

delighted
dependable
dependent
depressed
desirable
despairing
desperate
determined
devastated
different
dirty
disappointed
discerning
discouraged
disgusted
disheartened
distant
distrustful
doubtful
down
dumb
eager
ecstatic
embarrassed
empty
energetic
enraged
enthusiastic
envious
exasperated
excited
exhausted
exuberant
faithful
fascinated
fat
fearful
festive

fine
foolish
forgiving
fragile
frantic
frazzled
friendly
frustrated
fulfilled
full
furious
generous
glad
good
grateful
great
grief
grounded
grumpy
guilty
happy
harassed
hateful
heartbroken
heartless
helpless
high
hopeful
hopeless
horrible
horrified
hostile
hot
humiliated
humorous
hungry
hurt
hysterical

ignored
ill
impatient
important
impotent
inadequate
incompetent
indecisive
indifferent
inferior
inhibited
innocent
innovative
insecure
insignificant
interested
intimate
intuitive
irate
irritated
isolated
jealous
joyful
joyous
jubilant
jumpy
lazy
light
lonely
lost
lovable
loved
love-struck
loving
low
loyal
lucky
mad

mean
melancholy
miserable
misunderstood
moody
muddled
naked
needed
needy
nervous
nice
normal
numb
nurturing
obligated
obstinate
okay
old
on edge
optimistic
outraged
overwhelmed
pained
panicky
paranoid
passionate
pathetic
peaceful
pensive
pessimistic
petulant
phony
pissed
playful
pleased
poisonous
powerful
prejudiced

preoccupied
pressured
pretty
protective
proud
provoked
prudish
puzzled
querulous
quiet
ready
rebellious
regretful
rejected
relaxed
relieved
reliant
remorseful
resentful
respected
restless
sad
safe
satisfied
secure
self-conscious
self-reliant
separated
serene
sexy
sheepish
shitty
shocked
shy
sick
sick and tired
silly
skeptical

small
smug
sorry
special
stimulated
strange
stressed
strong
stubborn
stuck
stupid
submissive
successful
supportive
sure
surprised
suspicious
sympathetic
taxing
tender
tense
terrible
terrified
thankful
thoughtful
threatened
thrilled
tired
touchy
trapped
troubled
trusted
ugly
unappreciated
unattractive
uncertain
uncomfortable
undecided

understanding
understood
uneasy
unfulfilled
unhappy
unique
unloved
upset
uptight
used
useless
valuable
victimized
violated
vulnerable
wanted
warm
weak
weary
well
weird
wishy-washy
withdrawn
witty
wonderful
worn-out
worried
worse
worthwhile
wrong
young
youthful
zealous
zen

APPENDIX II: SELF-CARE SUGGESTIONS

Here are some ideas to get you started on the path to regular self-care.

- regular physical and dental checkups
- read novels
- treat yourself to a matinee
- journal or blog
- take walks
- coffee dates with friends
- massage
- laugh
- tai chi
- yoga
- cycling
- feeding the birds, bird watching
- gardening, landscaping
- artistic expression—painting, collage, needlework, etc.
- volunteer
- spend time with a pet
- do nothing—mindfully
- dance
- take yourself on a date
- practice technology sabbaticals
- eat fresh, healthy foods
- practice reasonable expectations
- seek out more laughter
- swim
- go out to dinner
- lie on the grass and gaze at the clouds
- get enough sleep
- hike
- watch the sunrise, the sunset, or both!
- listen to music
- play an instrument just for fun
- sing in the shower
- do a girls' or guys' night out
- build something
- de-clutter your house
- go on vacation
- go on a spiritual or personal development retreat
- work with a therapist, life coach, or spiritual director
- practice non-judgment
- write down five things a day you're grateful for
- set an intention to express your gratitude to others
- join a group—a dinner club, a book club, a writers' group, a running club, etc.
- meditate
- take a class for fun

APPENDIX III: GINGERBREAD MAN OUTLINE

APPENDIX IV: STOPLIGHTS

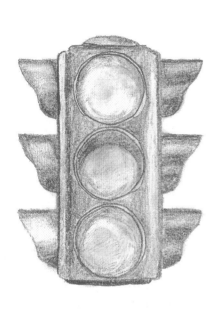
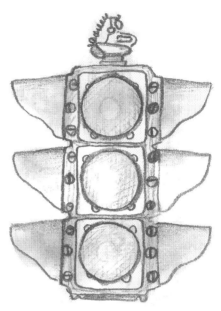

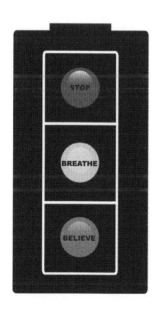

Bibliography

Amen, D. G. (1998). *Change your brain, change your life: the revolutionary, scientifically proven program for mastering your moods, conquering your anxieties and obsessions, and taming your temper.* New York: Times Books.

Ariely, D. (2012). *The (honest) truth about dishonesty: how we lie to everyone—especially others.* New York: Harper.

Augsburger, D. (1982). *Caring enough to hear and be heard.* Harrisonburg, VA: Herald Press.

Barton, R. R. (2006). *Sacred rhythms: arranging our lives for spiritual transformation.* Downers Grove, Ill.: InterVarsity Press.

Beattie, M. (1987). *Codependent no more: how to stop controlling others and start caring for yourself.* Center City, MN: Harper/Hazelden.

Beattie, M. (1990). *The language of letting go.* Center City, MN: Hazelden.

Benner, D. G. (2004). *The gift of being yourself: the sacred call to self-discovery.* Downers Grove, IL: InterVarsity Press.

Benson, H., & Proctor, W. (2010). *Relaxation revolution: enhancing your personal health through the science and genetics of mind body healing.* New York: Scribner.

Bly, R. (1990). *Iron John: a book about men.* Reading, Mass.: Addison-Wesley.

Brammer, R. (2011). *Diveristy in counseling (counseling diverse populations).* Belmont, CA: Brooks/Cole.

Brown, B. (2009). *Connections: a 12-session psychoeducational shame-resilience curriculum* (Rev. and expanded. ed.). Center City, MN: Hazelden.

Brown, C. B. (20082007). *I thought it was just me (but it isn't): telling the truth about perfectionism, inadequacy, and power*. New York: Gotham Books.

Brown, C. B. (2010). *The gifts of imperfection: let go of who you think you're supposed to be and embrace who you are*. Center City, MN: Hazelden.

Brown, C. B. (2012). *Daring greatly: how the courage to be vulnerable transforms the way we live, love, parent, and lead*. New York: Gotham Books.

Cain, S. (2012). *Quiet: the power of introverts in a world that can't stop talking*. New York: Crown Publishers.

Campbell, J. (1968). *The hero with a thousand faces* (2.ed.).: Princeton, (N.J.): Princeton University Press.

Campbell, J., Moyers, B.D. (1988). *The power of myth*. New York: Doubleday.

Davidson, R. J., & Begley, S. (20132012). *The emotional life of your brain: how its unique patterns affect the way you think, feel, and live--and how you can change them*. New York: Plume.

Dearing, R. L., & Tangney, J. P. (Eds.). (2011). *Shame in the therapy hour*. Washington, DC: American Psychological Association.

Donohue, J. (1997). *Anam cara: a book of Celtic wisdom*. New York: Cliff Street Books.

Gilbert, E. (2006). *Eat, pray, love: one woman's search for everything*. New York: Penguin Books.

Goleman, D. (1995). *Emotional intelligence*. New York: Bantam Books.

Gottman, J. M., & Silver, N. (1999). *The seven principles for making marriage work*. New York: Crown Publishers.

Hargrave, T. D., & Pfitzer, F. (2011). *Restoration therapy: understanding and guiding healing in marriage and family therapy*. New York: Routledge.

Harris, R. (2008). *The happiness trap: how to stop struggling and start living*. Boston: Trumpeter.

Herman, J. L. (1997). *Trauma and recovery* (Rev. ed.). New York: BasicBooks.

Jones, D. (2013). ~~I'm fine~~: *a real feelings journal*. Charleston: printed by CreateSpace.

Julian of Norwich (1966). *Revelations of divine love*. New York: Penguin Classics.

Jung, C. G., & Franz, M. (1964). *Man and his symbols*. Garden City, N.Y.: Doubleday.

Krueger, D. W., & Mann, J. D. (2009). *The secret language of money: how to make smarter financial decisions and lead a richer life*. New York: McGraw-Hill.

Lamott, A. (1999). *Traveling mercies: some thoughts on faith*. New York: Pantheon Books.

Lindahl, K. (2003). *Practicing the sacred art of listening: a guide to enrich your ela-tionships and kindle your spiritual life—the Listening Center workshop*. Woodstock, VT: SkyLight Paths Pub..

Melton, G. D. (2013). *Carry on, warrior: thoughts on life unarmed*. New York: Scribner.

Montgomery, A. (2013). *Neurobiology essentials for clinicians: what every therapist needs to know*. New York: W.W. Norton.

Neff, K. (2011). *Self-compassion: stop beating yourself up and leave insecurity behind*. New York: William Morrow.

Nepo, M. (2000). *The book of awakening: having the life you want by being present to the life you have*. Berkeley, CA: Conari Press.

Nepo, M. (2005). *The exquisite risk: daring to live an authentic life*. New York: Three Rivers Press.

Nouwen, H. J. (1988). *The road to daybreak: a spiritual journey*. New York: Doubleday.

Nouwen, H. J. (1996). *The inner voice of love: a journey through anguish to freedom*. New York: Doubleday.

Nouwen, Henri. (2004). *Out of solitude: three meditations on the christian life*. Notre Dame, IN: Ave Maria Press

Oliver, M. (1992). *New and selected poems*. Boston: Beacon Press.

Quinn, J. F. (1999). *I am a woman finding my voice: celebrating the extraordinary blessings of being a woman*. New York: Eagle Brook.

Real, T. (1997). *I don't want to talk about it: overcoming the secret legacy of male depression*. New York: Scribner.

Rilke, R.M., Kappus, F. X., & Burnham, J.M. (2000). *Letters to a young poet*. Novato, California: New World Library.

Rohr, R., & Martos, J. (1992). *The wild man's journey: reflections on male spirituality*. Cincinnati, Ohio: St. Anthony Messenger Press.

Scazzero, P. (2006). *Emotionally healthy spirituality: unleash a revolution in your life in Christ*. Nashville, TN: Integrity.

Segal, Z. V., Williams, J. M., & Teasdale, J. D. (2002). *Mindfulness-based cognitive therapy for depression: a new approach to preventing relapse*. New York: Guilford Press.

Siegel, D. J. (2010). *Mindsight: the new science of personal transformation*. New York: Bantam Books.

Siegel, D. J. (2012). *Pocket guide to interpersonal neurobiology: an integrative handbook of the mind* (1. ed.). New York: W.W. Norton & Co..

Siegel, D. J. (2013). *Brainstorm the power and purpose of the teenage brain*. New York: Jeremy P. Tarcher/Penguin.

Smith, D. B. (2012). *Monkey mind: a memoir of anxiety*. New York: Simon & Schuster.

Steinbaum, S., & Adamson, E. (2013). *Dr. Suzanne Steinbaum's heart book: every woman's guide to a heart-healthy life*. New York: Avery.

Stockett, K. (2009). *The help*. New York: Amy Einhorn Books.

Tolle, E. (1999). *The power of now: a guide to spiritual enlightenment*. Novato, CA: New World Library.

Williams, Margery. (1999). *The velveteen rabbit*. New York: Harper Collins.

Notes

[1] For more on this fascinating subject, see the work of Timothy D. Wilson or Suzanne J. Blackmore. Or of course, the grandfather of theories on the unconscious, Sigmund Freud.

[2] Siegel, D.J. (2010). *Mindsight: the new science of personal transformation.* New York: Bantam Books, 5.

[3] Ibid., 39.

[4] http://prtl.uhcl.edu/portal/page/portal/COS/Self_Help_and_Handouts/ Files_and_Documents/Abdominal%20Breathing.pdf.

[5] http://www.usaweekend.com/article/20130712/MONEY01/307120006/ I-ll-take-that-that-that-Experts-explain-impulse-buying.

[6] Ibid.

[7] Ibid.

[8] Smith, D. B. (2012). *Monkey mind: a memoir of anxiety.* New York: Simon & Schuster, 206.

[9] Brown, C.B. (2012). *Daring greatly: how the courage to be vulnerable transforms the way we live, love, parent, and lead.* New York, NY: Gotham Books, 72.

[10] Julian of Norwich, *Revelations of Divine Love*, Penguin Classics Edition, 2009, 103.

[11] Gilbert, E. (2006). *Eat, pray, love: one woman's search for everything across Italy, India and Indonesia*, 178.

[12] Ibid., 178-79.

[13] Siegel, D. *Mindsight*, 23.

[14] For a short video of Dr. Siegel explaining the hand model of the brain, see http://www.youtube.com/watch?v=DD-lfP1FBFk. The full, written explanation of the model can be found in *Mindsight*, pages 14-22.

[15] Ibid., *Mindsight*, 14.

[16] Ibid., 16.

[17] Ibid., 17.

[18] Ibid., 21.

[19] Ibid.

[20] Siegel, D. *Mindsight*, 26.

[21] Ibid., 28.

[22] I gave Michael some suggestions for reading on this theme, including Joseph Campbell's *The Hero with a Thousand Faces* and *The Power of Myth*, Robert Bly's *Iron John*, Richard Rohr's *The Wild Man's Journey*, and Carl Jung's *Man and His Symbols*. Information on each of these books can be found in the Bibliography.

[23] Which is not to be confused with what has been referred to as *competitive* suffering, or the habit some people have of always trying to "one up" others' stories of suffering.

[24] The boating accident occurred on December 14, 1996. Bob, Philip, Patrick, and Ben will be missed and remembered forever. The healing of such a loss is not on a timetable, but Helen continues to live life with a beautiful heart and an admirable strength. In a recent conversation with her, she recalled our conversation the week after the accident, when we spoke of Jeremiah 29:11 and of God's plans for us and the struggle *and* hope we have with faith amidst a tragedy. I was once again amazed at Helen's strength, her faith, her honesty about her hurt, and her ability to cling to hope amidst the pain of loss. Her life is an inspiration for all who hear her story.

[25] Oliver, M. (1992-2005). The Summer Day. *New and selected poems*. Boston: Beacon Press, 94.

[26] Neff, K. (2011). *Self-compassion: stop beating yourself up and leave insecurity behind*. New York: William Morrow, 42.

[27] The original line is "You is kind, you is smart. You is important." Stockett, K. (2009). *The help*. New York: Putnam, 443.

[28] http://www.nytimes.com/2013/02/10/opinion/sunday/relax-youll-be-more-productive.html?pagewanted=all&_r=0.

[29] Ibid.

[30] http://www.cnn.com/2011/HEALTH/01/05/touching.makes.you.healthier.health/index.html.
http://www.mayoclinic.com/health/massage/SA00082.

[31] Brown, C.B. (2007). *I thought it was just me (but it isn't): telling the truth about perfectionism, inadequacy, and power.* New York: Gotham Books, 145.

[32] To learn more about laughter yoga, visit www.laughteryogausa.com, www.laughteryoga.org, or www.laughinglaura.com.

[33] I am indebted to the invaluable research of Dr. Brené Brown for much of my understanding of shame and its effects. A full listing of Dr. Brown's books can be found in the bibliography.

[34] Brown, C.B. *Daring greatly*, 68-69.

[35] http://brenebrown.com/2013/03/20/2013320meuitdwaubpgr9qt1x-anm3fwwa0sjo/.

[36] Brown, C.B. *Daring greatly*, 69.

[37] Nouwen, Henri. *The Inner Voice of Love*, 38-39.

[38] Brown, Brene. DVD handouts, p. 42 Connections Curriculum.

[39] Williams, Margery. (1999). *The velveteen rabbit.* New York: HarperCollins, 13.

[40] www.spectrumthefilm.com

[41] Here are just a few stories, from both popular and scholarly resources, including the infamous case that happened in my own backyard of the dental assistant who was fired for being too attractive: http://www.huffingtonpost.com/2013/07/12/iowa-supreme-court-attractive-woman-firing_n_3586861.html; http://www.washingtonpost.com/wp-dyn/content/article/2010/05/20/AR2010052002298.html; http://www.psychologytoday.com/blog/games-primates-play/201203/the-truth-about-why-beautiful-people-are-more-successful; http://news.rice.edu/2011/11/09/looks-do-matter-2/; http://bit.ly/1g7x2nq.

[42] http://www.thebeautycompany.co/downloads/Beyer_BeautyNumbers.pdf.

[43] http://www.mint.com/blog/consumer-iq/splurge-vs-save-which-beauty-products-are-worth-the-extra-cost-0413/?display=wide.

[44] http://www.ywca.org/atf/cf/%7B711d5519-9e3c-4362-b753-ad138b5d-352c%7D/BEAUTY-AT-ANY-COST.PDF.

[45] Tragically, eating disorders in tweens and even elementary school children are becoming more prevalent. For a clinical study see http://pediatrics.aappublications.org/content/126/6/1240.full; thousands of "layperson" articles on eating disorders in children and adolescents are readily available on the Internet. If you suspect your child might have an eating disorder, please consult your pediatrician immediately.

46 Tolle, E. (1999). *The power of now: a guide to spiritual enlightenment.* Novato, Calif.: New World Library, 142.

47 Donohue, J. (1997). *Anam cara: a book of Celtic wisdom.* New York: Cliff Street Books, 104.

48 Lamott, A. (1999). *Traveling mercies: some thoughts on faith.* New York: Pantheon Books, 239.

49 http://www.phoenix-society.org/aboutus/history/.

50 Rohr, Richard. The CAC Foundation Set. http://store.cac.org/CAC-Foundation-Set-CD_p_65.html.

51 The full Feedback Format is far more in-depth, and can be found at http://www.themeadows.com/alumni-association/resources/listening-and-feedback-format.

52 Augsburger, David. (1982). *Caring enough to hear and be heard.* Harrisonburg, VA: Herald Press, 12.

53 http://www.jsonline.com/news/iraq/yoga-deep-breathing-used-to-address-soldiers-posttraumatic-stress-rs6fuh4-166332636.html.

54 There are many guides to relaxation and breathing practices available. An excellent introductory guide comes from the Trauma Center at Justice Resource Institute; these exercises were designed to help the victims and responders of the 9/11 terrorist attacks. The guide may be found at http://www.traumacenter.org/resources/pdf_files/relaxation_exercises.pdf.

55 Kim's full story unfolded over several sessions; the following account is a compressed version of her sharing.

56 Siegel, Daniel. *Mindsight*, 187.

57 Nouwen, Henri. (2004). *Out of solitude: three meditations on the christian life.* Notre Dame, IN: Ave Maria Press, 38.

58 Rilke, R. M., Kappus, F. X., & Burnham, J. M. (2000). *Letters to a young poet.* Novato, Calif.: New World Library, 21.

59 http://www.essentiallifeskills.net/williamjamesquotes.html.

About the Team

Dianne Morris Jones is a Licensed Mental Health Counselor (LMHC) and a Certified Daring Way™ Facilitator-Consultant (CDWF-C) practicing at Family Legacy Counseling in Des Moines, Iowa. Dianne is the author of ~~I'm Fine~~: *A Real Feelings Journal.* She has a degree in Family Finance from Texas Tech University and a Master's degree in Counseling from West Texas A&M University. Dianne is an energetic and creative person who approaches life and her professional counseling with an enthusiasm for growth in wholehearted living. She practices individual and couples therapy from a mindful, cognitive behavioral approach. Her clinical focus includes depression, anxiety, relationship issues, trauma, and life transitions. In addition to being a Certified Laughter Yoga Instructor, Dianne has extensive training in Spiritual Direction and the Enneagram. She speaks frequently on the joys and challenges of choosing to live life in an intentional, authentic way. When Dianne is not in the office, she enjoys outdoor adventures, photography and spending time with friends and her adult children, Justin and Jill. Dianne and her husband Roger live in West Des Moines, Iowa.

ↂ

Catherine Knepper is a freelance editor and writer. Her clients' books have been published by Berkley Books, Bloomsbury, Broadway, Crown, Oxford University Press, Permanent Press, Perseus Books, Progressive Press, Random House, Rodale Books, Rowman & Littlefield, St. Martin's Press, Sarabande Books, Hudson Street Press and various university and independent presses. A graduate of the Boston University School of Theology and the Iowa Writers' Workshop, she lives in Des Moines, Iowa with her husband Tim and two children James and Frances.

ↂ

Monica Ghali is an aspiring recognizer and creator of beautiful things and a lover of story. Her work in Lima, Peru in the nonprofit sector pushed her to face into many interesting challenges and experience the world in a new way. She is now living in Omaha, Nebraska where she is a fellow at the Union for Contemporary Art, soaking in the wisdom of the creative community, and working as a freelance graphic designer.

ALSO BY DIANNE MORRIS JONES

I'm Fine. A Real Feelings Journal invites you to move past the "I'm fine" response we reflexively give to the question of how we are and instead recognize and express our authentic emotional experience. Prompts on the right side of the journal offer you an opportunity to explore specific feelings through words, and the journal's blank left side allows you to communicate your feelings through drawing, collages, doodling, or any other artistic expression. To accompany you on this important journey into inner awareness, *I'm Fine* offers inspiring quotes, a comprehensive list of feeling words, reflections to ponder, and a guide for further exploration through the lens of *The Guest House* by Rumi. Work and play through this journal on your own or find a partner or group for discussion and community. *I'm Fine* is a wonderful way to gain a deeper understanding of your deepest heart and soul and move steadily toward a life of greater authenticity and vulnerability.

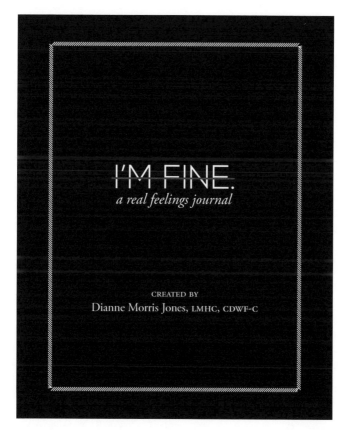

Made in the USA
Columbia, SC
25 March 2018